Hand Drafting
for INTERIOR DESIGN

Diana Bennett Wirtz

ASID, IIDA
ART INSTITUTE OF SEATTLE

FAIRCHILD
BOOKS

NEW YORK

Executive Editor: Olga T. Kontzias
Assistant Acquisitions Editor: Amanda Breccia
Editorial Development Director: Jennifer Crane
Associate Art Director: Erin Fitzsimmons
Production Director: Ginger Hillman
Production Editor: Jessica Rozler
Cover Design: Erin Fitzsimmons
Interior Illustrations and Cover Art: Diana Bennett Wirtz

Second Printing 2010
Third Printing 2011

Library of Congress Catalog Card Number: 2008939615
ISBN: 978-1-56367-737-3
GST R 133004424
Printed in the United States of America
TP09

Hand Drafting
for INTERIOR DESIGN

fb

CONTENTS

Preface xiii

Acknowledgments xiii

CHAPTER one Drafting Tools 1

CHAPTER two Lettering 19

CHAPTER three Windows, Walls, and Doors in a Floor Plan 31

CHAPTER four Furniture in a Floor Plan 43

CHAPTER five Flooring in a Floor Plan 61

CHAPTER six Kitchens and Baths 73

CHAPTER seven Architectural Details in a Floor Plan 91

CHAPTER eight Interior Elevations 103

CHAPTER nine Exterior Elevations 115

CHAPTER ten Sections 137

Glossary 141

EXTENDED CONTENTS

Preface   xiii

Acknowledgments   xiii

Chapter One, Drafting Tools   1

Drafting Tools and How to Use Them   3

    Architect's Scale   3

    Six-Inch Architect's Scale   3

    T-Squares, Parallel Rules, and Drafting Arms   4

    Parallel Bar   4

    Drafting Arm   5

    Drafting Boards   5

    Drafting Tables   6

    Triangles   6

    Compass   8

    Templates   8

    Erasers   9

    Drafting Brushes   10

    Pencils   10

        Uses for Different Lead Weights   11

        Lead Holders   12

        Mechanical Pencils   12

        Wood Pencils   12

        Pencil Line Weight   13

        Types of Lines   13

    Drafting Vellum   14

My Favorite Tools   14

    Erasing Shield   14

    Sanding Block   14

    Kneaded Erasers   15

Design of Title Blocks   16

[EXTENDED CONTENTS]

Chapter Two, Lettering   19

Basic Block   21

    Upper   22

    Lower   22

        More Variations   23

        Still More Variations   24

        And More   25

    Bold Lettering   26

    Bold Numbers   27

    Some Yes's   28

    Some No's   29

Chapter Three, Windows, Walls, and Doors in a Floor Plan   31

Drawing Windows   33

Walls   34

    Interior Design Walls   35

Drawing Doors   37

    French Doors   38

    Sliding Doors   38

    Bifold Doors   39

    Pocket Doors   40

    Another Pocket Door   40

Additional Doors   41

Windows, Walls, and Doors   42

Chapter Four, Furniture in a Floor Plan   43

Chairs   45

    More Square Chairs   46

    Smaller Square Chairs   47

    Club Chair/Office Chair   48

    Chair Variation   49

    Drawing Sofas   50

    Sofa Variety   51

    More Sofas   52

    And More Sofa Styles   53

Drawing Tables with Chairs   54

Other Tables with Chairs   55

Office Furniture   56

More Office Furniture   57

Drawing Beds   58

      Bed Design Ideas   59

Additional Furniture   60

Chapter Five, Flooring in a Floor Plan   61

Tile Flooring   63

More Tile Flooring   64

Additional Tile Flooring   65

Granite and Concrete   66

Flooring and Paving   67

      Wood Flooring   68

      Old World Wood Flooring   69

            More World Flooring   70

      Fun Wood Flooring   71

      Carpeting   72

Chapter Six, Kitchens and Baths   73

The L-Shaped Kitchen   75

Corridor Kitchens   76

U-Shaped Kitchen   77

One-Wall Kitchen   77

Height Requirements, Space Requirements   78

Standard Sizes, Standard Heights–Cabinets   79

Switch Symbols   80

      Receptacle Symbols Continued   81

      Lighting Symbols Continued   82

Kitchen Appliances   83

      Kitchen Appliances Continued   84

Typical Kitchen Reflected Ceiling   85

Kitchen Elevations   86

Basic Bath Layouts   87

      Basic Bath Layouts Continued   88

Bathrooms   89

More Tub & Shower Techniques   90

[EXTENDED CONTENTS]

Chapter Seven, Architectural Details in a Floor Plan   91

Architectural Details   93

    Architectural Details Continued   94

Area Rugs   95

    Area Rug Ideas   96

    Simpler Area Rugs   96

    Some Fun Area Rugs   97

Plants   98

    More Plant Designs   99

    Plant Variations   100

        More Plant Variations   101

        And More   102

Chapter Eight, Interior Elevations   103

Drawing Elevations   105

Furniture in Elevation   106

Drawing Windows   107

    Windows   108

        More Windows Looking Out   109

    Window Coverings   110

        More Window Coverings   111

    Draperies   112

One Wall, Different Styles   113

    And More Styles   114

Chapter Nine, Exterior Elevations   115

Exterior Elevations   117

Exterior Elevation   118

Exterior Siding   119

Siding   120

    Siding Shadows   121

    Siding Continued   122

    Siding Continued   123

    Siding Continued   124

    Siding Continued   125

Siding Continued   126

Siding Options   127

Roof Details   128

Roof Details Continued   129

Roof Variations   130

More Roof Ideas   131

Exterior Trees   132

Trees Continued   133

Trees Continued   134

Trees Continued   135

Trees in Front   136

Chapter Ten, Sections   137

Building Section   139

Definition by Line Weight   140

Glossary   141

PREFACE

Hand Drafting for Interior Designers is about the process of learning to draft in a beautiful manner using the right tools. Writing a simple book of beautiful hand drafting techniques has always been a vision of mine. I learned wonderful style and techniques from many of my college design professors and wanted to pass the style and beauty on to a broader audience than just my current students. While computer-aided design (CAD) is an enhancement to designing, drafting continues to be the most efficient way to learn architectural principles. It is my endeavor that CAD students can add the beautiful hand rendering style I demonstrate in this book to their CAD drawings to make them more personal and artistic. This drafting style can be done in pencil or in ink. It is the basis of beautiful drawing. You can take simple drawings, define and delineate them, and your clients will enjoy your presentations. Because design is about 94 percent sales, if you cannot sell your design to your clients, you are not really designing. This book will give you many of the tools needed to do just that.

Acknowledgments

As we go through our lives we should take the opportunity to reflect on the people who have influenced our lives, loved us unconditionally, and had the wisdom and fortitude to mentor us that we might succeed in ways we never imagined. I have led a gifted life in many ways being surrounded by many wonderful people.

My father, Ralph Wilson Bennett, who died when I was just sixteen, always told me I could do whatever I thought I could in life. When I was in college I thought I should marry a doctor or a lawyer who drove a Porsche. After finishing my BA in Art, I met my late husband, Frederick Richard Wirtz, a partner with Gibson, Dunn & Crutcher law firm, who met both qualifications (lawyer and Porsche driver). He became my best friend, a brilliant father to my sons, and my knight and mentor. He insisted I complete my master's degree, pass the NCIDQ, and become the professional interior designer I had dreamed of becoming while growing up on a farm in rural Northern California.

I loved hand drafting and drawing, taking many classes over the years, and I had wonderful college professors who encouraged me to always excel. Raising my three sons, Chadwyck, Kyle, and Maxx, after the death of my husband, forced me to work hard in order to succeed and be able to offer them opportunities as they were growing into adults. I was lucky to be able to teach, practice design, paint, and sell real estate over the years. Thank you for all the best friends and mentors a person could ask to have in life.

CHAPTER ONE

DRAFTING TOOLS

As interior designers we need to be able to transform the creative ideas and plans in our minds into reality. In order to do this we have to be able to effectively communicate those ideas and plans to others. Using the "tools of the trade" described in this chapter, interior designers can bring their wonderful ideas to the rest of the world by drafting them by hand on paper.

Drafting Tools and How to Use Them

The first step in the process is learning which tools you need to have in order to get started. If you buy good tools in the beginning, your tools will last a lifetime. In this chapter you will learn about the "tools of the trade" for drafting, including the pencils and proper pencil weights used for hand drafting in contemporary design.

Tools of the trade include:

1. Architect's scale
2. T-square, parallel rule, or drafting machine
3. Drafting board
4. Triangles
5. Compass
6. Templates
7. Erasers
8. Drafting brush
9. Pencils, wood or mechanical pencils
10. Tracing vellum
11. Sanding block
12. Kneaded eraser

Architect's Scale

An architect's scale is used to accurately measure and scale a drawing in feet and inches. The major divisions are $\frac{3}{32}$, $\frac{1}{16}$, $\frac{1}{8}$, $\frac{3}{16}$, $\frac{1}{4}$, $\frac{3}{8}$, $\frac{1}{2}$, $\frac{3}{4}$, 1, $1\frac{1}{2}$, and 3. Each one of these divisions represents one foot on the scale in that scale size. For example, in the $\frac{1}{4}$-inch scale, one quarter of an inch on the scale represents one foot. When you use the scale, begin counting off the feet at the 0 point. The inches are scaled on the other side of the 0 point.

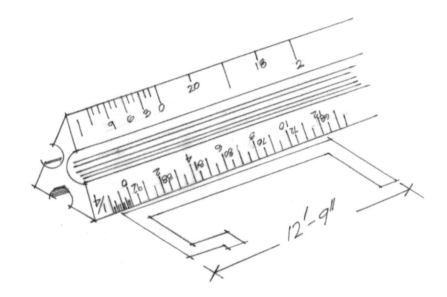

 Note: The scale only looks complicated; it actually is very simple once you start using it. I like to take a permanent marker and mark the $\frac{1}{4}$-inch scale so that I can see which side of the scale I'm using more easily when working.

Six-Inch Architect's Scale

The 6-inch architect's scale is a small, simple scale to use. I find it great to use when laying out floor plans. Using this smaller size scale takes away the confusion of flipping the larger scale.

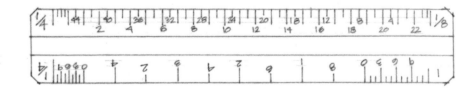

T-Squares, Parallel Rules, and Drafting Arms

T-squares come in different lengths, from 18 inches to 48 inches. Pick the one that is appropriate to the board or table you are using to draft. T-squares are fairly inexpensive and come in either metal or wood with a see-through plastic edge. They need to be held in place while you are drawing, because the end farthest from the angle may move a bit if you do not hold it. The T-square is portable, which makes it convenient for design students.

Note: If your drafting board is a little cracked on the edge, line up your paper with the edge of the board and your drawing will be straight.

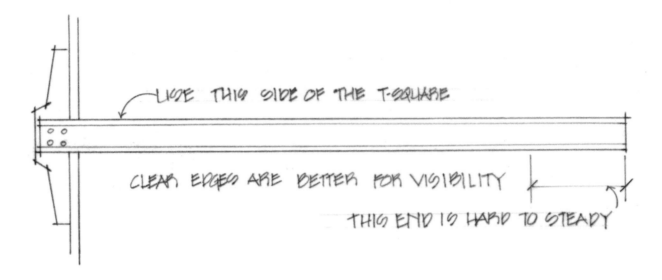

USE THIS SIDE OF THE T-SQUARE

CLEAR EDGES ARE BETTER FOR VISIBILITY

THIS END IS HARD TO STEADY

Parallel Bar

Because they are easier to keep in place, the parallel bar (also called the parallel rule) and the drafting arm can be used in place of a T-square. The parallel bar is attached to a drafting board with a system of pulleys and cables, allowing the straight edge to move up and down the board in a parallel manner. It is

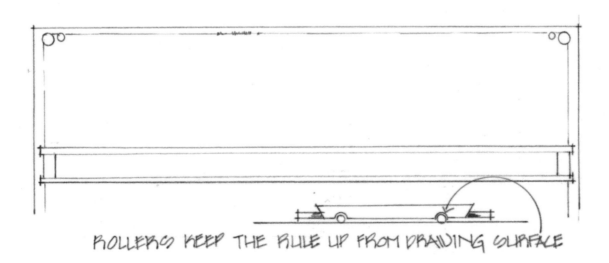

ROLLERS KEEP THE RULE UP FROM DRAWING SURFACE

always parallel to the top of the board. The parallel rule is easy to use, and it allows the person drafting to move the bar up and down and draft in a faster manner than using the T-square. Like T-squares, parallel rules also are available in a variety of lengths from 30 inches to 60 inches.

Rollers permit the parallel rule to move easily across the drafting surface. Clear acrylic edges make it easy to see the lines you have drawn.

Drafting Arm

Drafting arms, also called drafting machines, combine the best of the T-square and the parallel rule. A drafting arm is attached to your drafting board or table. It has built-in scales on the horizontal and vertical blades, so you do not have to have a separate architect's scale for measuring. Drafting machines are made for left- and right-handed people. You can rotate the head by pressing and releasing the lock and use the arm at angles, similar to how a triangle is used.

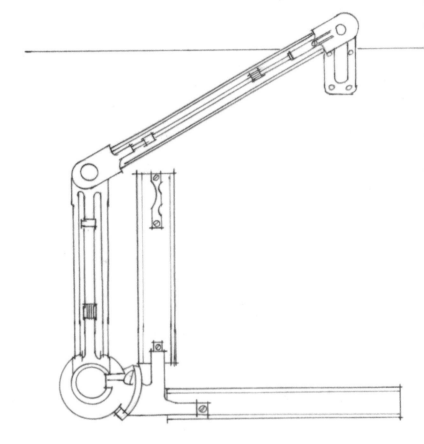

There are two types of drafting arms:
- The *arm type* has two arms that rotate in the middle, extended from an arm that is clamped to the top of your board or table.
- The *track type* is attached to the board at the top of the board with a horizontal bar across the top with a vertical track attached that slides to the left and right.

Note: In using a parallel rule when I first started drafting on a board that I carried back and forth to class, I found the cables would become loose and the bar would have to be tightened often to try to keep it straight. I switched back to a T-square and then invested in a drafting machine, also called a drafting arm, in my office.

Drafting Boards

Drafting boards come in a wide variety of shapes and sizes. Schools often suggest that students have a lightweight board to carry back and forth to class. At home, a drafting table or drafting stand is a better solution. A drafting stand has an adjustable top, so that you can work at an angle comfortable for you. Search the Internet and you likely will find the size you want.

Note: I like to cover the top of my drafting table with Borco™ (Trademark registered with Safco Products Co., Minneapolis, Minnesota). It is a vinyl cover that is stain-resistant, easy on the eyes, and "self-healing" for your pencil lines.

Drafting Tables

Drafting tables are also available in a wide variety of sizes, materials, and shapes. They usually have a shallow drawer on one side.

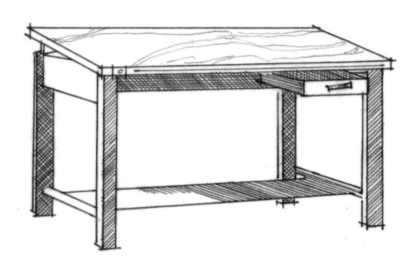

Triangles

Triangles generally are made out of clear, scratch-resistant acrylic and provide a clear, undistorted view to your drawing. Triangles come in a variety of sizes: 45/90-degree, 30/60-degree, and, my favorite, the adjustable triangle, which can adjust from 0 to 45 degrees.

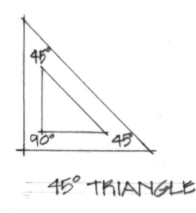

45° TRIANGLE

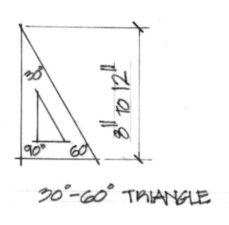

30°-60° TRIANGLE

Note: The size of the triangle is determined by the length of the longest side of the right angle.

The adjustable triangle is held in place by a thumbscrew with a movable arm. Line up the scales in the middle to make different angles. The adjustable triangle is convenient for a variety of sloping lines, such as angled furniture or stairs.

Large triangles are great for drawing long vertical lines perpendicular to the edge of the T-square. Small triangles are perfect for lettering or for the detailed hatch marks in drawings.

You can combine triangles to draw longer lines or parallel lines. You also can combine triangles to draw different angles, but I find the adjustable triangle works best for this.

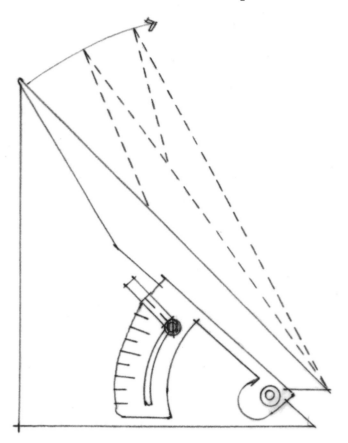

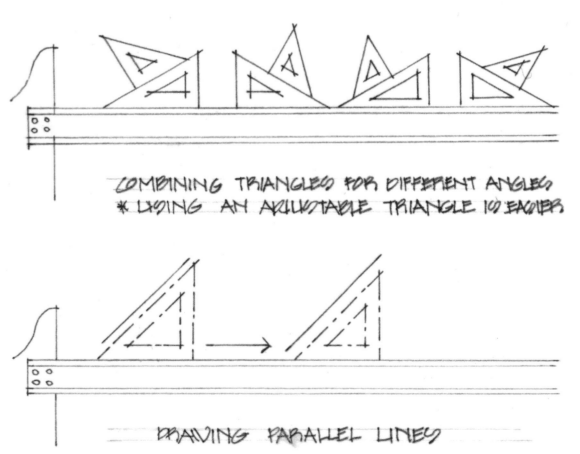

COMBINING TRIANGLES FOR DIFFERENT ANGLES
* USING AN ADJUSTABLE TRIANGLE IS EASIER

DRAWING PARALLEL LINES

[DRAFTING TOOLS]

Compass

Compasses are needed in order to draw large circles. Circle templates work best for smaller circles because you have more control of your lead pressure. It can be difficult to apply even pressure using a compass. A chisel point for your compass pencil works best in an F lead. An H lead or harder will produce too light a line.

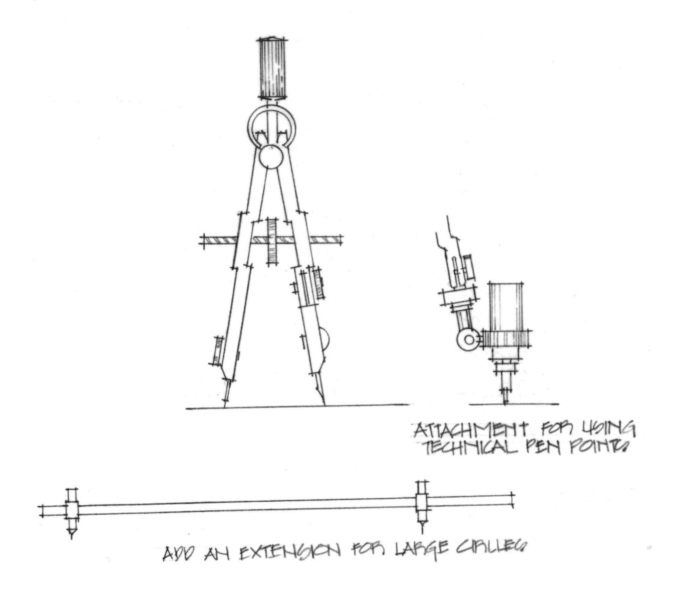

ATTACHMENT FOR USING TECHNICAL PEN POINTS

ADD AN EXTENSION FOR LARGE CIRCLES

An extension arm can be added for larger circles.

Templates

Templates, made of acrylic with cutouts of predetermined shapes, are useful when beginning your layouts. Circle templates, for example, have circles of graduated sizes. They can be used for door swings, tables, artwork, laying out plants, as well as a variety of other elements in drawings. There are templates for kitchen equipment, bath equipment, living room furniture, bedroom furniture, office furniture, and ellipses. Templates are available in ⅛-inch scale and ¼-inch scale for architectural drawings. Many beginning design students go no further in the drawing process than using templates to show furniture and equipment in the floor plan. Templates are just the beginning. Templates should be used as a guide to help place furniture in the floor plan. A designer should then draw the furniture and the details using the techniques illustrated in this book, using beautiful and delicate hand drafting.

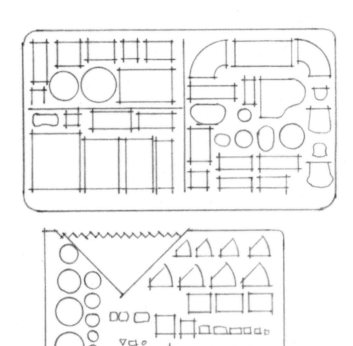

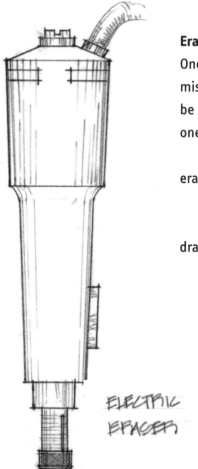

ELECTRIC ERASER

Erasers

One of the wonderful advantages of pencil drafting is being able to erase mistakes. One of the disadvantages of pencil drafting is that not all lines can be easily erased. Erasers come in a variety of shapes and sizes. Try different ones to see what works best for your style.

A good electric eraser could be your new best friend. Battery-operated erasers and rechargeable erasers are also available.

Kneaded erasers work great in large areas.

Pink Pearl and White Vinyl erasers are available in art supply and drafting supply stores.

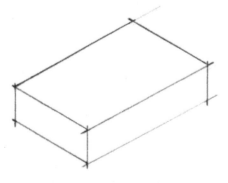

PINK PEARL OR WHITE VINYL ERASERS

The erasing shield may be a small piece of equipment, but it can play a big role in your design drawing process. The erasing shield is a small rectangle of metal with various shaped holes, intended to be placed over your drawing in progress to isolate and eliminate your mistakes. It is effective in protecting your drawing while using an electric eraser.

Drafting Brushes

Keeping the surface of your drawing clean is of the utmost importance. Every time you erase, you need to use your drafting brush to clean off the extra graphite. I find the softer the brush, the easier it is to keep clean.

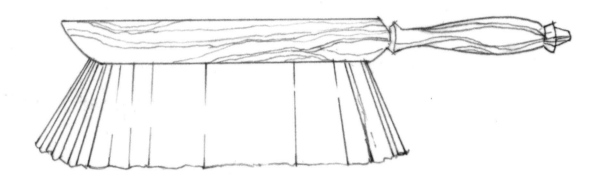

Drafting powder can be used as a protective coating over drawings while drafting. But drafting powder can be tricky, in that if you use too much, your lines may skip. It can be safer and easier to put a piece of tracing paper over the part you have completed.

Pencils

There are many types of drafting pencils that can successfully be used for drafting. Pencils weights range from 9H to 6B, as shown on the chart below.

Hard								Medium						Soft
9H	8H	6H	4H	3H	2H	H	F	HB	B	2B	3B	4B	5B	6B

Pencils used for design drafting are usually 4H to B. Anything harder will tear the vellum and anything softer will smudge too easily.

Uses for Different Lead Weights

4H

4H lead is hard and dense and great for initial layout of drawings where you are going to fill in later with more detail. The lines will be light and hard to read and not reproduce well in finished drawings. People who have a "heavy hand" can carefully use this lead for details. If it is applied too intensely, it will tear the vellum or leave marks on your drafting table.

2H

2H lead is great for filling in details in a drawing. It is suitable for finished drawings, but only if used with some pressure. If too light pressure is used, it will not show up, too much pressure and you can tear the vellum. Use this lead weight to draw detail in furniture and to *poché* (to fill in) the walls in floor plans. If drawn with a heavy hand, 2H is difficult to erase.

H

H lead pencil is superb for the detail lines in drawings. H can be used to darken windows or mirrors, as will be shown in upcoming chapters. It also can be used to fill in walls, if you do not have a heavy hand, and draw in details on area rugs, plants, or any other object of interest.

F

F lead pencil is my favorite pencil. You can use it to make the darkest lines without much smudging, if carefully applied. Use the F pencil for lettering, walls, and outside lines on furniture in finished drawings.

HB

HB was used more when everything was blue printed, as it can show up as quite dark. It can be used for dense line-work or hand lettering, but it will also easily smudge, so should not be used without great care.

B

B lead is very soft and can make impressive dark lines. It is better used for sketching and drawing than drafting.

Lead Holders

Lead holders use 2mm leads that can be drawn out or pulled back by the push-button on the end control-ling the length of the lead. The lead can be contracted when not in use. The different lead weights can be used in any lead holder. The point of the lead will be sharpened with a lead pointer.

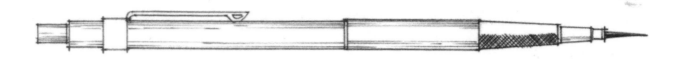

Mechanical Pencils

Mechanical pencils use 0.3 mm, 0.5 mm, 0.7 mm, and 0.9 mm leads:

• 0.3 mm are for fine lines but they do break easily
• 0.5 mm are used most often as they are hardier
• 0.7 mm and 0.9 mm are better for sketching and lettering

Mechanical pencils work with the same push-button mechanism as lead holders. The mechanical pencils hold thin leads that do not need to be sharpened. I feel that mechanical pencils do not allow for as much control of your lines, however, and so prefer to use wood pencils.

Wood Pencils

Wood pencils have always been my choice for drafting. I feel that by actually touching the pencil, you are more in touch with your drafting. There are many brands of wood pencils available; try several different ones to see which is most comfortable in your hand and produces the best lines for you. For example, Mars Staedtler Lumograph has been my brand of preference for many years. You do have to sharpen your pencil every few strokes. In the past it was recommended to sharpen to a long (¾") thin point, and then use a lead pointer or sandpaper to refine the point even more. I find a good electric pencil sharpener works best.

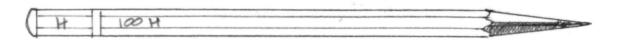

Of course, it is a personal preference as to which style of pencil you use for your drafted drawings. Used correctly, all three—wood, mechanical, or lead holder—can produce beautiful quality in line drawings. Try out each style and see what feels best to you personally.

Note: Be sure to rotate your pencil between your thumb and forefinger as you are drafting long lines, and apply an even and steady pressure. It will give you a cleaner and neater line without the fuzzy lines that most beginning drafting students always have. And be sure to sharpen your pencil at least twice as often as you think you should.

Pencil Line Weight

Lines and the use of them is the essence of drafting. It is important to know what different lines represent in the art of drafting. If you understand the use of the different lines, you will have an easier time drawing all your plans and anyone reading them should be able to understand.

All lines should be uniformly dense, not fuzzy, so they are easier to read and will reproduce the same. Each pencil lead produces a slightly different weight of line. Pencils can vary from one brand to the next within the same pencil weight. For example, a Berol Turquoise H pencil might be slightly different than a Mars Staedtler Lumograph H pencil.

SOLID OUTSIDE LINE

DETAIL LINE

SUPPLEMENTARY DETAILS

DASHED LINES

CENTER LINE

GRID LINES

MAJOR LINES
F OR H

Types of Lines

Solid lines define the form of objects, such as the outside line of a floor plan. The darker the line, the more the space is defined.

Dashed lines indicate essentials hidden from view. The upper cabinets in a kitchen would be shown this way.

Centerlines, shown by long lines, then short dashes or long dots, show the axis.

Grid lines drawn with a light hand in H or 2H pencil are great for setting up tile and wood floors.

SECONDARY LINES
H OR 2H

GRID OR LAYOUT LINES
H, 2H, OR 4H

Drafting Vellum

Drafting vellum is a high-quality transparent paper that is easily drawn on with pencils and from which drawings can be erased without great difficulty. Reproductions can be made from pencil drawings on drafting vellum. The paper also takes ink well, without bleeding.

My Favorite Tools

There are several tools that I personally use on a daily basis to make my drafting quicker, neater, and more efficient. My favorites of these tools are described below.

Erasing Shield

One of the puzzles of beginning drafting is the erasing shield, an item of which beginning drafters never see the value. Erasing shields come in various sizes and shapes, are invaluable once you know how to use them, and they are very simple! The thin, stainless steel shields

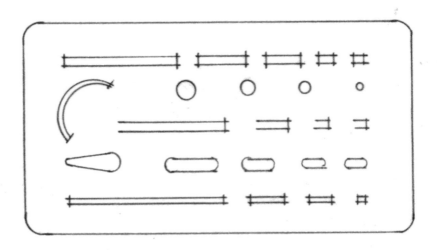

effectively protect the drawing surface while you use the electric eraser to erase defined areas. I love it, because you can easily and effectively correct your own mistakes.

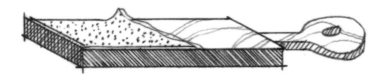

Sanding Block

The sanding block is a piece of wood with sandpaper sheets stapled to the end. It is used to obtain a tapered, conical point on your pencil or angle the end of the point for lettering. The point of your pencil, whether mechanical or lead holder or wood, makes the difference in drawing and particularly in lettering—the point of your pencil needs to be angled to do excellent lettering.

Do not let your pencil get too dull, or you will have fuzzy line quality. You can use the sanding block between sharpening to keep a very sharp point.

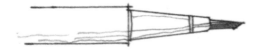 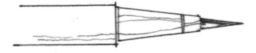 

Kneaded Erasers

My favorite eraser is a Kneaded Rubber Eraser by Banford. To clean it, you have to pull and stretch. Kneaded erasers are great for cleaning surfaces.

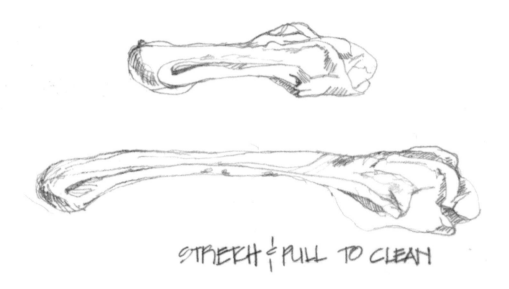

STRECH & PULL TO CLEAN

. . . And a trick about rolling your drawings.

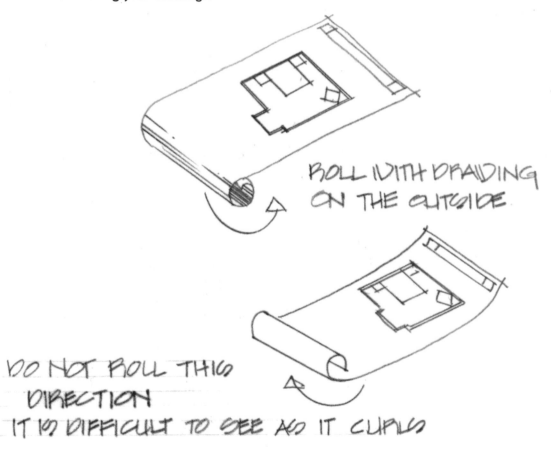

ROLL WITH DRAWING ON THE OUTSIDE

DO NOT ROLL THIS DIRECTION
IT IS DIFFICULT TO SEE AS IT CURLS

Design of Title Blocks

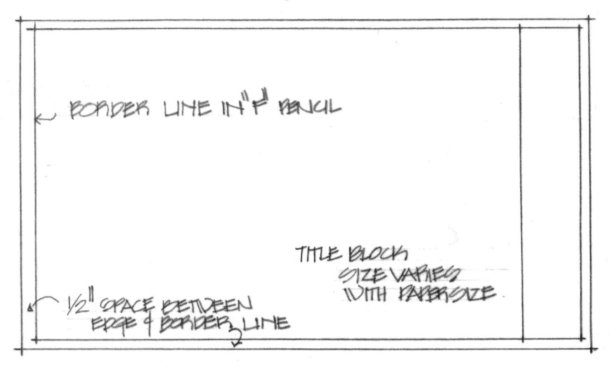

BORDER LINE IN "F" PENCIL

TITLE BLOCK
SIZE VARIES
WITH PAPER SIZE

½" SPACE BETWEEN
EDGE & BORDER LINE

NOTE: TITLE BLOCK IS ON EVERY PAGE OF DOCUMENTS

Title blocks should be simple and clearly define what you are drawing. Generally title blocks appear at the bottom or the right-hand side of the drawing. A title block can be drawn horizontally or vertically.

A title block should include the following information:
- Name of design firm—This should be in a large font, including the logo, address, and other contact information
- Artist or designer—Include name and contact information
- Title of project—Include project title, location information, and client/owner, if applicable
- Scale—Note the scale of the drawing, e.g., ¼-inch, etc.
- Draftsperson—If the draftsperson was someone other than designer, include his or her initials
- Date—Give the date the initial drawing was created
- Revision dates—Include six spaces for names and dates of revisions
- Client approval—Include space for the signature of the client to indicate approval of the document as drawn
- Sheet Title—This usually is a short title indicating the specific name of the drawing(s) on that page, e.g., "floor plan," "elevation," etc.
- Sheet number—There could be up to 50 drawings or more for any given project.

DESIGN FIRM
  ADDRESS
  ADDRESS
  PHONE #
  EMAIL
  WEBSITE

DESIGNER

PROJECT

REVISIONS
  DATE   DRAWN BY

CLIENT APPROVAL

FIRST FLOOR PLAN
  SCALE: 1/4"=1'-0"

SHEET NUMBER A1

17

CHAPTER two

here are entire books written solely on lettering. Good lettering can make the difference between a merely acceptable presentation and an impressive one. Professional lettering styles should be taught and practiced from the beginning of the study of interior design. There is a range of lettering styles that are suitable to use in conjunction with hand drafting. Well-executed and artistically drawn lettering can mean gaining entrée to the professional office of your preference, or not.

Universal Notes on Lettering

This chapter will show you the basics of good lettering and then some variety of that lettering. We should begin with some universal notes on lettering:

- Lettering should be all uppercase (caps).
- Lettering should always be drawn with a top and bottom guideline for uniformity.
  - A well-sharpened 4H pencil works well for guidelines because it is a hard pencil and can make a very thin line.
  - Guidelines never need be erased; they become part of the design.
- One-eighth-inch lettering is considered standard.
- Space between lines should also be $\frac{1}{8}$ of an inch.
- Use a triangle for vertical lines on lettering more than $\frac{1}{8}$ of an inch.
- Your freehand lettering will improve with practice.
- Curvy or playful lettering is inappropriate.
- Use an Ames Lettering guide to set guidelines.
- One-quarter-inch or block lettering is used in title blocks for client description.
- It is accepted practice in lettering to have the vertical stroke thin and the horizontal thicker. This is explained in more detail later in this chapter.

Finding your own lettering style is fun, as you try many different styles within the suitable range till you find one that works well for you. This chapter begins by illustrating basic block lettering. If you learn basic block lettering in the beginning, you can then adapt and change it to your style or to the style of the design firm where you work. Lettering is like anything else: if you understand how it works first, you can make it your own later.

BASIC BLOCK

ABCDEFGHIJKLMNO PQRSTUVWXYZ

ALL THE LETTERS ARE BASICALLY SQUARE AND THE SAME SIZE. W AND M ARE A LITTLE WIDER.

FROM THIS BASIC FORMAT YOU CAN ADD WHAT I CALL "PERSONALITY."

NOTE:
DO NOT ADD TAILS TO I OR J IN A SIMPLE BLOCK

I J

OR ANY ARCHITECTURAL LETTERING.

PERSONALITY MIGHT BE MOVING THE CENTER LINE UP OR DOWN.

FORM EVER FOLLOWS FUNCTION

FORM EVER FOLLOWS FUNCTION.
LOUIS HENRY SULLIVAN

DO NOT VARY WITHIN EACH STYLE.
UPPER VERSUS LOWER

UPPER
A B C D E F G H I J K L M N O
P Q R S T U V W X Y Z
NOTE THE B, K, P, R, AND S CENTER LINE.

LOWER
A B C D E F G H I J K L M N
O P Q R S T U V W X Y Z
NOTE THE SAME LETTERS WITH LOWER.

ANOTHER WAY TO CHANGE THE BASIC BLOCK
IS MAKE THE HORIZONTAL LINES AT A SLANT.

A B C D E F G H I J K L M N O
P Q R S T U V W X Y Z

NOTES
- KEEP THE ANGLE OF THE SLANT CONSISTENT
- THE Z DOES NOT ANGLE Z TOO CUTE
- VERTICAL LINES SHOULD TOUCH GUIDELINES

ALL ART IS BUT IMITATION
OF NATURE.
                    LUCIUS ANNAEUS SENECA

MORE VARIATIONS

SLANTING THE LETTERS GIVES A DIFFERENT LOOK. KEEPING THE ANGLE THE SAME IS THE DIFFICULT PART.

ANOTHER VERSION MAKES THE STRAIGHT LINE LETTERS THIN AND THE ROUND LETTERS WIDE. THE ROUND LETTERS CAN BE A BIT LARGER.

A B C D E F G H I J K L M N O P Q
R S T U V W X Y Z

FRANK LLOYD WRIGHT
USED WIDE SPACING AND
NARROW STRAIGHT LINES
AND WIDE ROUND LETTERS
SIMILAR TO ABOVE.

HE ALSO DESIGNED ART DECO FONTS
A B C D E F G H I J K L M N O
P Q R S T U V W X Y Z

DIANA'S STYLE

MY PERSONAL STYLE IS A COMBINATION OF SEVERAL STYLES.

A B C D E F G H I J K L M
N O P Q R S T U V W X Y Z

MORE VARIATIONS
ABCDEFGHIJKLMNOPQRS
TUVWXYZ 1234567890

+ NOTE IT DOES NOT TAKE MUCH TO CHANGE A STYLE.

STUDENTS OFTEN LIKE TO ADD LOTS OF CURVES
ABCDEFGHIJKLMNOPQRST
UVWXYZ 1234567890

THIS IS NOT A STYLE I RECOMMEND!

STUDENTS OFTEN DESIGN ALPHABETS WITH A
WIDE RANGE OF DEVIATION. IN DESIGNING
YOUR LETTERING BE SURE ALL YOUR LETTERS ARE
COHESIVE.

HERE IS ANOTHER STYLE YOU
MIGHT WANT TO ADAPT TO USE.

ABCDEFGHIJKMNOPQRS
TUVWXYZ 123456789

SOME MERELY CHANGE THE LOOK BY EXTENDING
AN OCCASIONAL LETTER, WHICH GIVES YOU A WHOLE
NEW LOOK.

YOU CAN HAVE FUN
WITH LETTERING.

AND MORE.

ABCDEFGHIJKLMNOPQRSTUVWXYZ
1234567890
LETTERING STYLE

ABCDEFGHIJKLMNOPQRSTUVWX
YZ   1234567
LETTERING STYLE
THIS IS A FUN AND DIFFERENT
STYLE.

HAVE FUN
WITH
YOUR STYLE.

25

BOLD LETTERING

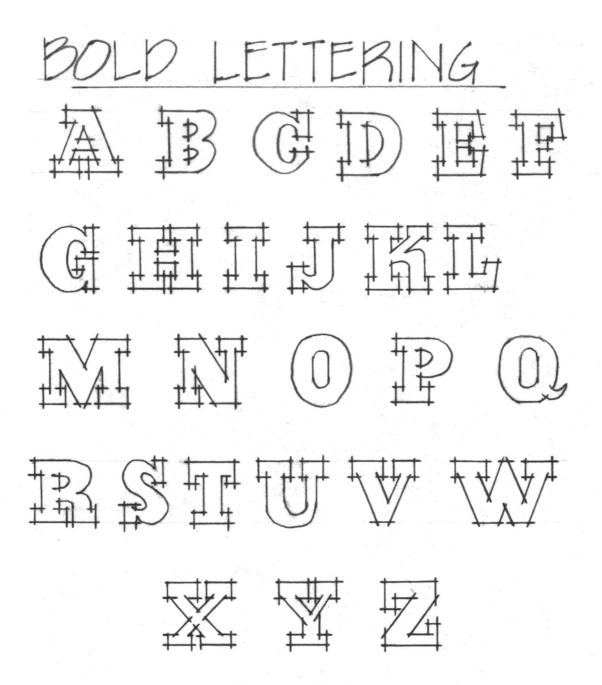

THE LETTERING SHOWN ABOVE CAN BE USED FOR
THE NAME OF THE PROJECT IN A TITLE BLOCK.
IT IS BEST TO TRACE LETTERS FORMING THE
NAME ON A SEPARATE PRACTICE SHEET FIRST.

BOLD NUMBERS

1 2 3 4 5 6

7 8 9 0

SOME YES's

- ALWAYS DRAW THE VERTICAL LINES FIRST WITH A CHISEL POINT
- THEN DRAW THE HORIZONTAL LINES WITH THE "FAT" PART OF THE CHISEL

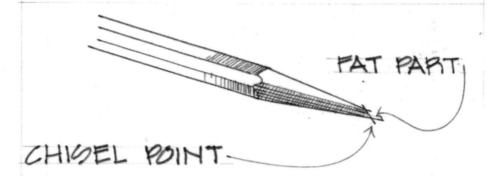

FAT PART

CHISEL POINT

- ADD EMPHASIS (DARKEN WITH PRESSURE) TO THE BEGINNING AND END OF EVERY LINE

ESPECIALLY WITH YOUR LETTERING

ABCDEFGHIJKLM

OR LOOKING AT A LARGER VIEW

A B C D E

NOTE EMPHASIS

SOME NO's

IN LETTERING NO's CAN ONLY BE SHOWN BY EXAMPLE:

- DON'T MAKE YOUR LETTERING
  TOO WIDE

- OR   TOO NARROW AND CLOSE

- OR   TOO CLOSE.

- AND NOT TOO SLOPPY

- PLUS DON'T DO YOUR LETTERING TILL LAST. IT WILL SMUDGE

AND DON'T FORGET TO PRACTICE!

CHAPTER **three**

WINDOWS, WALLS, AND DOORS IN A FLOOR PLAN

indows, walls, and doors must be drawn on the floor plan in a uniform manner that is legible, simple, and easily understood. This chapter includes step-by-step illustrations of how to draw a selection of windows, walls, and doors generally used in interior design and construction.

As an interior designer I have often designed re-models and additions for my clients. Once my design is complete, if there are any walls moved, I always hire an engineer or knowledgeable contractor to make sure that I am not moving any load-bearing walls.

This is a very simple chapter, but it is very necessary to be precise.

DRAWING WINDOWS

WINDOWS ARE BEST DRAWN IN A SIMPLE MANNER.

FIXED WINDOWS

DRAW THE WALL FIRST USING "F" PENCIL.
A FIXED WINDOW IS DEPICTED WITH ONE LINE
IN THE CENTER USING PENCIL "H"

DOUBLE HUNG WINDOWS

DRAWN THE SAME AS FIXED WINDOWS WITH
TWO LINES DRAWN IN THE CENTER IN "H"

WINDOW WITH SILL

DRAWN AS ABOVE WITH EXTENDED SILL

BAY WINDOW

WALLS

WALLS ARE DRAWN A BIT SIMPLER IN AN INTERIOR DESIGN DRAWING THAN IN A SET OF ARCHITECTURAL DOCUMENTS.

WALLS ARE GENERALLY DRAWN AT 6 INCHES. PLUMBING WALLS ARE DRAWN AT 9 INCHES.

CONSTRUCTION WALLS

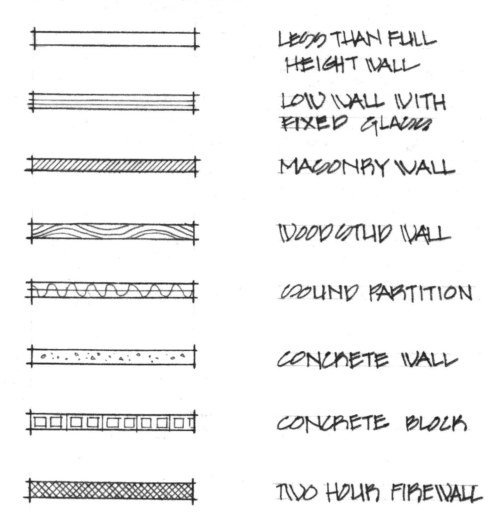

LESS THAN FULL HEIGHT WALL

LOW WALL WITH FIXED GLASS

MASONRY WALL

WOOD STUD WALL

SOUND PARTITION

CONCRETE WALL

CONCRETE BLOCK

TWO HOUR FIREWALL

INTERIOR DESIGN WALLS

DRAWINGS USED FOR PRESENTATION BY INTERIOR DESIGNERS COMMONLY POCHE' THE WALLS

POCHE' — LITERALLY MEANS 'POCKET' IN FRENCH. IN INTERIOR DESIGN DRAWINGS WE FILL IN THE POCKET OF THE WALLS IN FLOOR PLANS FOR IMPROVED READABILITY.

HOW TO POCHE'
DRAW THE WALL IN 'F' PENCIL. FILL IN WITH FINE LINES IN 'H' OR '2H'.

YES —

DON'T MAKE THE LINES TOO DARK OR TOO FAR APART.

NO —

SEE THE DIFFERENCE. THE FIRST ONE DRAWN LOOKS MUCH BETTER.

DRAWING CORNERS

DRAW A 45° ANGLE IN THE CORNER VERY LIGHTLY.

DRAW LINES TO MEET AT THE ANGLE.

MAKE EMPHASIS AT BEGINNING & END.

35

POCHE' OF INTERIOR CORNERS

BUTT THE SHORTER
WALL OF POCHE' INTO
THE LONGER WALL.

ANOTHER STYLE OF POCHE'

THIS IS A FREER-LOOKING STYLE DONE FREE HAND.

TOTAL POCHE' FILL IN

THIS STYLE SEEMS TOO PLAIN OR BORING
TO ME PERSONALLY.

DRAWING DOORS

DRAW THE WALL VERY LIGHTLY IN 4H PENCIL.
MEASURE TO PLACE THE DOOR.

DRAW THE WALL WITH YOUR F PENCIL.

THE DOOR IS DRAWN THE SAME AS THE WIDTH OF
THE OPENING. IF THE DOOR IS 3'-0" WIDE, THE
DOOR IS DRAWN 3'-0" LONG.

THE DOOR IS DRAWN USING THE H PENCIL.
THE DOOR IS DRAWN AT 2" DEEP FITTING INSIDE
THE OPENING.

THE DOOR SWING IS DRAWN USING A CIRCLE
TEMPLATE WITH H PENCIL.

FRENCH DOORS

FRENCH DOORS ARE DRAWN THE SAME AS SINGLE
DOORS. THE DOOR SWINGS MUST BE CENTERED

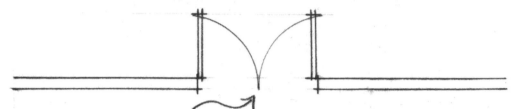

NOTE THAT THE SWING IS DRAWN TO THE
BOTTOM OF THE WALL.

* CROSS CORNERS AS SHOWN

SLIDING DOORS

ONCE AGAIN DRAW THE WALL AND MEASURE
THE DOOR OPENING. WALLS ARE GENERALLY
DRAWN AS 6" THICK.

DRAW THE CENTER FIRST.

DIVIDE IN HALF AND DRAW EACH SIDE OF THE DOOR.
TRY TO DRAW THEM BOTH AS EVENLY AS YOU CAN.

ANOTHER STYLE OF SLIDING DOORS

BIFOLD DOORS

BIFOLD DOORS CAN BE DRAWN IN SEVERAL DIFFERENT WAYS.

45 DEGREES
THE DOORS ARE AT 45°.

FIGURE THE WIDTH OF EACH DOOR AND DRAW IT THE PROPER SIZE.

12.5 DEGREES

THE IDEA IS THE SAME, BUT PRODUCES A DIFFERENT LOOK.

ONE SIDE CLOSED

ACCORDION FOLDING

IDENTICAL TO BIFOLD DOORS WITH SHORTER SECTIONS

POCKET DOORS

THE OPENING IN THE WALL MUST BE THE SAME
DEPTH AS THE WIDTH OF THE DOOR.

$$\frac{1}{4}'' = 1'-0''$$

DRAW THE WALL AND THE DOOR FIRST, THEN
ADD THE OPENING IN THE WALL FOR THE
DOOR TO GO INTO.

$$\frac{1}{4}'' = 1'-0''$$

ANOTHER POCKET DOOR

POCKET DOORS CAN BE DRAWN IN MORE
THAN ONE MANNER.

ADDITIONAL DOORS

DOUBLE SWINGING DOORS GO BOTH DIRECTIONS.

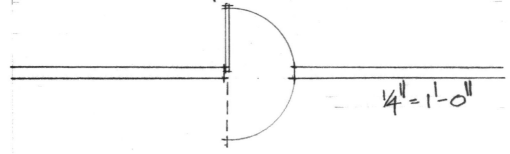

$\frac{1}{4}" = 1'-0"$

REVOLVING DOORS

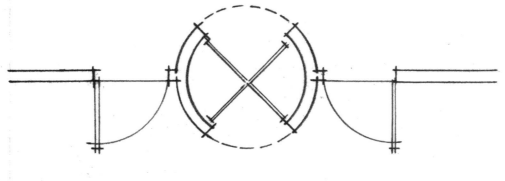

CASED OPENING

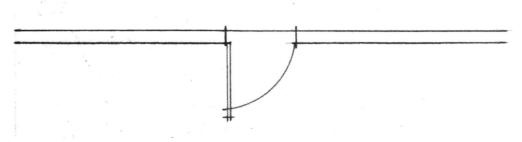

EXTERIOR DOOR

WINDOW, WALLS & DOORS

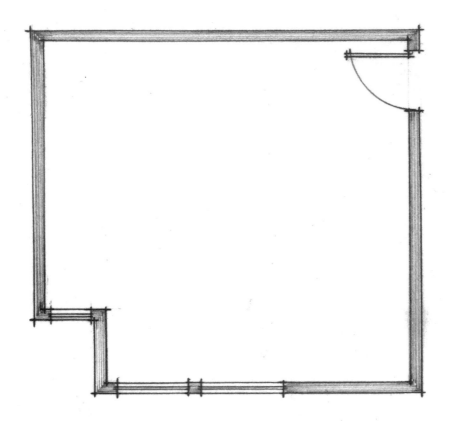

NOTES

1. OUTSIDE WALL IS DARKEST "F" PENCIL.

2. POCHE' THE INSIDE OF THE WALLS LIGHTER. YOU CAN USE AN "H" OR "2H" LEAD.

3. DOORS AND WINDOWS ARE DRAWN USING AN "H" OR "2H" LEAD.

4. DOOR SWING IS DRAWN USING A CIRCLE TEMPLATE AND A "H" OR "2H" LEAD.

CHAPTER four

FURNITURE IN A FLOOR PLAN

You must be a successful salesperson to be a winning designer. If you cannot sell your ideas or your designs to your client, are you a designer? Drawing furniture in your floor plans in a presentation style takes your drawings from very plain to striking.

This chapter, as well as the following chapters, will show you how to draw interior floor plans and elevations as small works of art. Your clients will be impressed by how well you have thought out and presented your ideas.

CHAIRS

MOST CHAIRS ARE 36" SQUARE.
DRAW A SQUARE USING YOUR T-SQUARE
AND TRIANGLE USING A 2H PENCIL.

OUTLINE THE RECTANGLE IN F PENCIL.
ADD A LINE IN 4H TO INDICATE CHAIR
BACK AND ONE FOR A PILLOW.

DRAW INSIDE LINES TO FORM CHAIR.
BE SURE TO CROSS CORNERS.

ADD THE BACK CUSHION FREEHAND.
DRAW IT AS A SOFTENED SQUARE.
THE LINES ACROSS THE CENTER ARE WELTING.

ADD A SOFT CURVE TO THE FRONT
IN FREEHAND.

ROUND THE CORNERS FREEHAND IN "F" PENCIL.

DRAW A QUARTER CIRCLE USING A CIRCLE
TEMPLATE. FILL IN WITH LINES USING "2H."

THIS LOOKS LIKE IT IS COMPLICATED
BUT IS FAST & SIMPLE.

MORE SQUARE CHAIRS

SHORTEN THE ARMS OF THE ORIGINAL DESIGN.

DRAW THE SAME CHAIR ROUNDING THE ENTIRE FRONT.

OR JUST ROUND THE CENTER OF THE CHAIR.

CUT IN BACK EITHER TOTALLY WITH DRAFTING EQUIPMENT OR PARTIALLY FREE HAND.

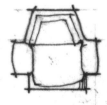

DRAW CLASSIC EAMES CHAIR PART FREE HAND. YOU CAN DRAW ANY CHAIR SMALLER OR LARGER.

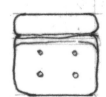

DRAW A KNOLL BARCELONA CHAIR WITH JUST A FEW LINES.

SMALLER SQUARE CHAIRS

SMALLER 24" CHAIR IN BLOCK STYLE WORKS FOR DINING ROOM.

MAKE CHAIRS DISTINCT WITH LITTLE MODIFICATIONS.

ADD A SHADOW.

ROUND THE ARMS AND ADD AN OTTOMAN TO MAKE A LOUNGE CHAIR.

DRAW FREEHAND WITH SHADOWS FOR A DIFFERENT LOOK.

ADD A BACK FOR AN OFFICE CHAIR.

OR ADD THE ILLUSION OF A BACK.

OR MAKE IT LOOK ATTACHED.

CLUB CHAIR / OFFICE CHAIR

CLUB CHAIRS ARE GENERALLY 36"
SO START WITH 3/4" CIRCLE IN 1/4"
SCALE. DRAW WITH 2H OR 4H.

DARKEN HALF OF THE CIRCLE WITH
'H' PENCIL.

EXTEND LINES TO EDGE OF CIRCLE.

DRAW ACROSS BOTTOM FORMING SHAPE.

DRAW INTERIOR TO CHAIR USING
A SMALLER CIRCLE AND EXTEND
TO THE FRONT LINE.

DRAW ANOTHER CIRCLE TO DRAW
SHADOW TO DEFINE THE CHAIR.

THE SHADOW CAN BE DRAWN
A COUPLE OF DIFFERENT WAYS.
NOTE THE EMPHASIS AT
THE BEGINNING AND END OF
EVERY LINE.

CHAIR VARIATION

ROUND THE FRONT OF THE CHAIR AND DRAW THE SHADOW BY HAND, THIS GIVES A SOFTER LOOK.

DRAW THE CHAIR SHORTER.

DRAW THE SAME CHAIR WITH STRAIGHT ARMS.

THE CHAIR CAN BE DRAWN SMALLER BY USING 1/2" CIRCLE ON THE CIRCLE TEMPLATE.

YOU CAN ADD ARMS AND SHADOWS FOR DIVERSITY.

EXTEND THE SIDES AT A 10 DEGREE ANGLE USING AN ADJUSTABLE TRIANGLE FOR A DIFFERENT LOOK.

ROUND THE LINES FOR ANOTHER LOOK AND ADD SHADING.

OR DON'T ADD SHADING.

49

DRAWING SOFAS

MOST SOFAS ARE 36" DEEP.
DRAW A RECTANGLE USING A "2H" PENCIL.
USE YOUR TRIANGLE AND T-SQUARE.

OUTLINE THE RECTANGLE IN "F" PENCIL.
ADD A LINE IN "4H" PENCIL TO INDICATE
SOFA BACK AND ONE FOR PILLOWS.

DRAW INSIDE LINES IN "H" PENCIL
TO FORM THE BACK OF THE SOFA.
BE SURE TO CROSS CORNERS.

DIVIDE INTO THREE SECTIONS OR
INTO TWO DEPENDING ON
SIZE OR DESIGN.

DRAW THE PILLOWS FREEHAND
USING THE "H" PENCIL.

ROUND THE CORNERS FREEHAND
USING "F" PENCIL.

DRAW AN ARCH USING A CIRCLE
TEMPLATE AND "H" PENCIL.
FINISH HARDLINE VERTICAL LINES.
THE SOFA IS COMPLETE.

SOFA VARIETY

YOUR SIMPLE SOFA CAN BE CHANGED AND SIMPLY BECOME INTERESTING.

DRAW THE OUTSIDE EDGE IN "F" PENCIL. ADD A LINE IN 4H PENCIL TO INDICATE SOFA BACK AND PILLOW ROW.

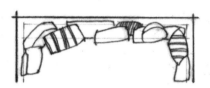

DRAW IN PILLOWS IN "H" PENCIL. HAVE FUN!

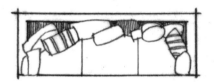

DIVIDE INTO THIRDS OR HALVES. DARKEN SPACES BEHIND PILLOWS.

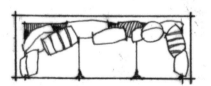

ROUND THE CORNERS FREEHAND IN "F."

LEAVE LIKE THIS OR ADD SHADOW.

DRAW THE ARCH IN "H" PENCIL. HARDLINE VERTICAL LINES. NOTE THE EMPHASIS ON THE CIRCLE END OF THE LINE. ——

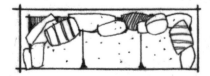

USE DOTS FOR TEXTURE.

MORE SOFAS

SECTIONAL - DRAW SIMILAR TO SOFAS

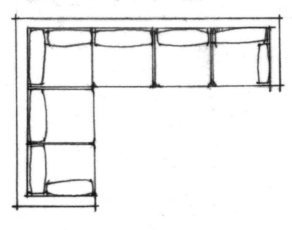

CHAISE

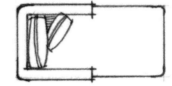

SOFA WITH CHAISE

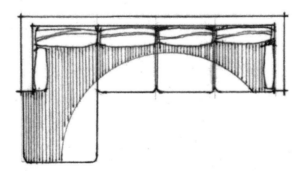

NOTE THE SHADOW ADDS
DEPTH TO THE DRAWING.

AND MORE SOFA STYLES

CIRCULAR SOFAS WORK IF YOU MAKE
THEM SPACIOUS ENOUGH FOR KNEE SPACE.

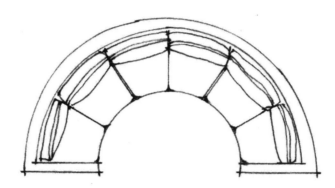

THIS SIZE WORKS.

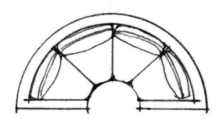

THIS SIZE DOES __NOT__ WORK. IT LOOKS
GOOD ON PAPER, BUT YOUR KNEES DO
NOT FIT IN THE MIDDLE.

HISTORICAL OR VICTORIAN

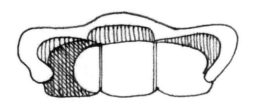

DRAWING TABLES WITH CHAIRS

CHAIRS AROUND A TABLE CAN BE SPACED
USING THE TECHNIQUE SHOWN BELOW.

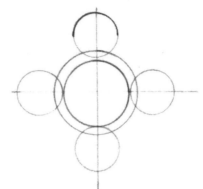

DRAW THE SPACING OF CHAIRS USING CIRCLES.

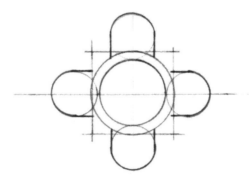

START TO ADD DETAIL.

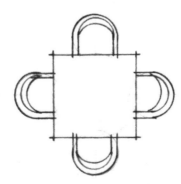

FINISH THE DETAIL ~ DO THIS THEN TRACE.

OTHER TABLES WITH CHAIRS

USE THE SAME TECHNIQUE FOR CHAIRS
THAT ARE NOT PARTLY UNDER THE TABLE.

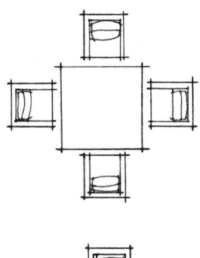

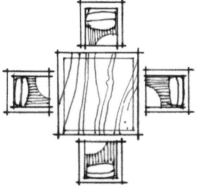

THEN HAVE FUN ADDING DETAIL.

OFFICE FURNITURE

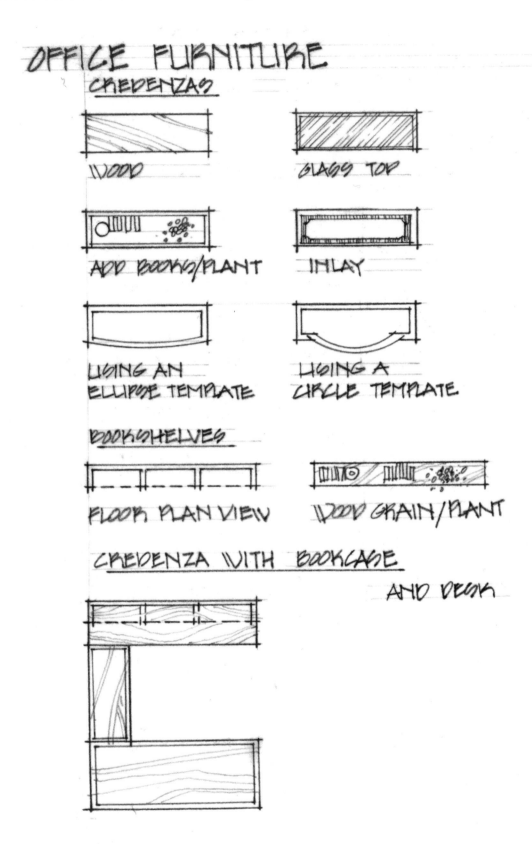

CREDENZAS

WOOD

GLASS TOP

ADD BOOKS/PLANT

INLAY

USING AN
ELLIPSE TEMPLATE

USING A
CIRCLE TEMPLATE

BOOKSHELVES

FLOOR PLAN VIEW

WOOD GRAIN/PLANT

CREDENZA WITH BOOKCASE

AND DESK

MORE OFFICE FURNITURE

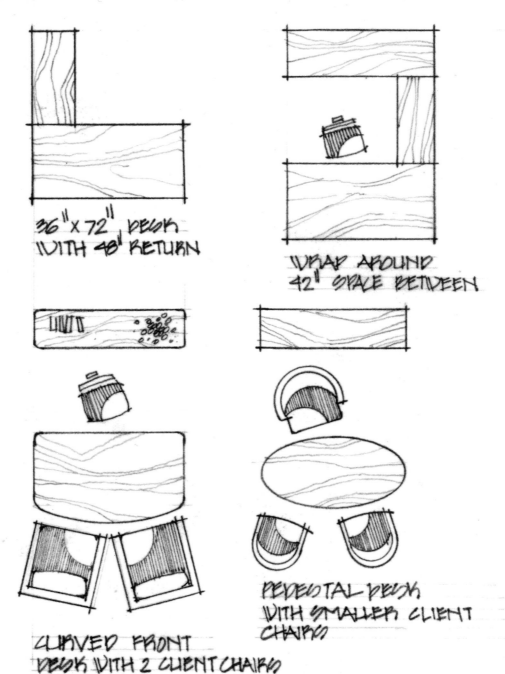

36"x 72" DESK
WITH 48" RETURN

WRAP AROUND
42" SPACE BETWEEN

CURVED FRONT
DESK WITH 2 CLIENT CHAIRS

PEDESTAL DESK
WITH SMALLER CLIENT
CHAIRS

DRAWING BEDS

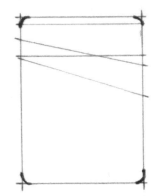

DRAW THE OUTLINE OF THE BED.
DRAW THE CORNER BY HAND.

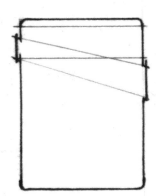

DARKEN IN THE OUTSIDE LINE.
NOTICE THE FOLD-DOWN AREA IS
EXTENDED.

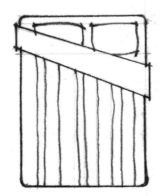

USE THE LINES TO DRAW IN THE
PILLOWS FREEHAND.
ADD DESIGN OF YOUR CHOICE.

BED DESIGN IDEAS

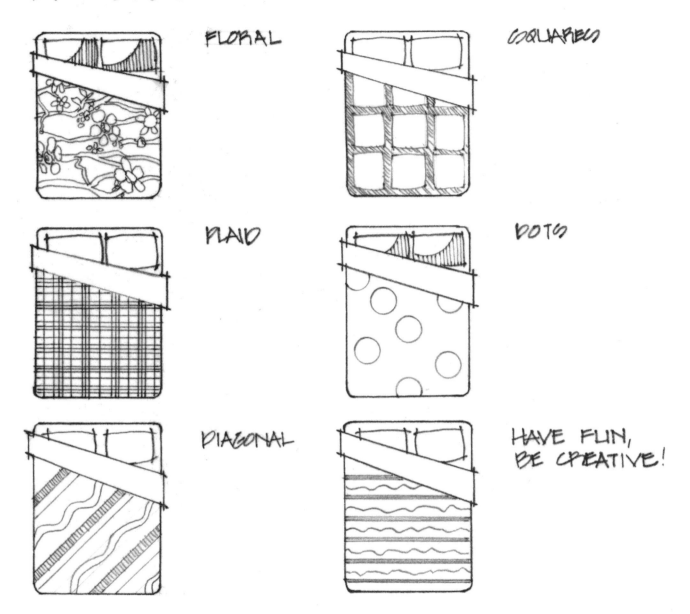

FLORAL

SQUARES

PLAID

DOTS

DIAGONAL

HAVE FUN,
BE CREATIVE!

ADDITIONAL FURNITURE

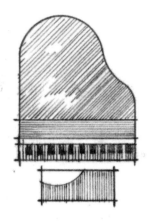 GRAND PIANO

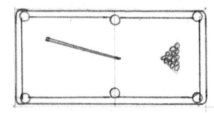 POOL TABLE

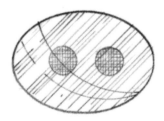 GLASS TOP TABLE

 ADIRONDACK CHAIR

CHAPTER five

FLOORING IN A FLOOR PLAN

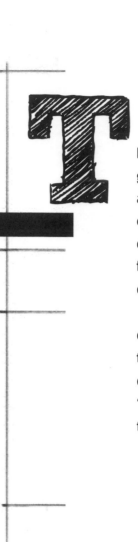

This chapter will illustrate how to draw interior flooring as a background using different tile and wood patterns, bamboo, concrete, and marble. Flooring in a presentation-style floor plan should be executed using a light hand, so that it does not overwhelm your drawing. Using a 2H or 4H pencil will enable you to illustrate the flooring design and texture without detracting from the overall drawing.

The exception to using a 2H or 4H in flooring is when drawing dots for carpeting. An F pencil should be used when drawing dots to show carpeting texture. One of the important factors in drawing dots to give texture to carpeting, or anything else, is *not* to draw "tails" on the dots. Examples of good and bad dots are included in this chapter.

TILE FLOORING

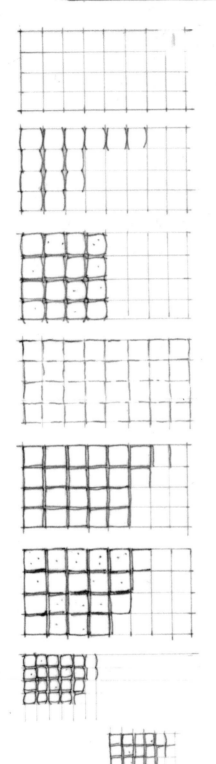

12" X 12" CAN BE DRAWN IN MANY WAYS.
DRAW A GRID IN ¼" SCALE LIGHTLY
WITH A 2H PENCIL.

12" X 12" TILES CAN BE ROUNDED FREEHAND.
DRAW THE VERTICAL LINES FIRST
USING A 2H PENCIL.

NEXT DRAW THE HORIZONTAL LINES
USING A 2H PENCIL.
ADD A FEW DOTS TO MAKE IT INTERESTING.
USE AN "F" PENCIL FOR THE DOTS.

12" X 12" TILE WITH SOFT LINE
DRAW THE VERTICAL FIRST IN 2H.
THEN DRAW HORIZONTALS.
SOFTLY BREAK THE LINES.

12" X 12" TILES CAN BE SQUARED FREEHAND
USING THE SAME TECHNIQUE AS DESCRIBED.
VERTICAL FIRST — THEN HORIZONTAL.
DRAW LINES STRAIGHT AS YOU CAN.

ADD DOTS FOR CHARACTER.
CONNECT SOME SQUARES.

8" X 8" TILES CAN BE DRAWN USING THE
SAME TECHNIQUES AS ABOVE
AND DETAILED THE SAME.

MORE TILE FLOORING

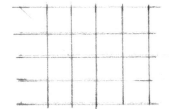

TILE CAN BE DRAWN IN A SIMPLE MANNER AND BE EFFECTIVE. ALWAYS BEGIN WITH A LIGHT GRID DRAWN WITH A 4H PENCIL.

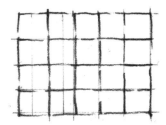

TRACE THE 4H GRID WITH 2H PENCIL WITH VARYING PRESSURE AND BREAKS IN THE LINES.

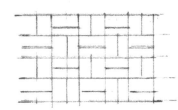

6" x 12" BASKET WEAVE BEGINS WITH A 12" x 12" GRID, DIVIDED AND DRAWN FREEHAND.

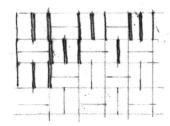

DRAW THE VERTICAL LINES FIRST. PLACE TWO LINES CLOSE TOGETHER TO SHOW GROUT LINES.

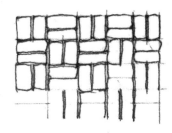

FINISH BY DRAWING THE HORIZONTAL LINES. THIS IS A FREE-HAND STYLE.

ADDITIONAL TILE FLOORING

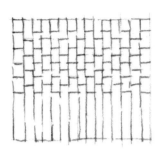

4" x 8" RUNNING BOND IS DRAWN OVER A 4" x 4" GRID FREEHAND.

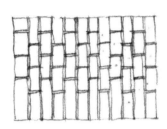

6" x 12" RUNNING BOND IS DRAWN IN A SIMILAR MANNER, ADDING DOUBLE LINES TO SHOW GROUT.

ADD DOTS FOR INTEREST.

NATURAL STONE FLOORS CAN BE A DYNAMIC ADDITION TO A DESIGN IF DONE CORRECTLY.

DO <u>NOT</u> DRAW ROCKS LIKE CIRCLES
DO <u>NOT</u> CONNECT WITH NO SPACE BETWEEN SHAPES.

GRANITE & CONCRETE

GRANITE IS AVAILABLE IN MANY
DIFFERENT LOOKS, FROM MEDIUM TO
COARSE TEXTURE.
& COARSE GRANITE

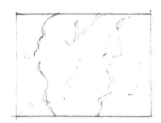

MEDIUM TEXTURE GRANITE CAN
BE DRAWN IN A SIMPLE MANNER.
& MEDIUM GRANITE

CONCRETE FLOORS TAKE MANY LOOKS.
MOST OFTEN THEY ARE DESIGNED WITH
EXPANSION JOINTS.

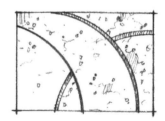

CONCRETE WITH EXPANSION JOINTS
CAN BE USED TO FORM PATTERNS.

CONCRETE DRAWN AS IN AN
OLD LOFT

FLOORING & PAVING

COBBLESTONE IS DRAWN WITH A VARIETY OF CIRCLES. CONNECT WITH SHORT LINES.

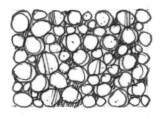

RECTANGULAR CUT STONE

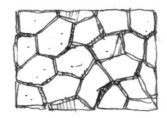

RANDOM FLAGSTONE MUST BE DRAWN AT THE RIGHT SCALE.

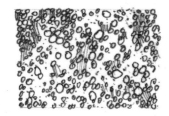

TERRAZZO CAN BE DRAWN AS PEBBLES.

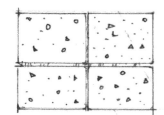

OR TERRAZZO CAN BE DRAWN AS SIMPLY AS SHOWN HERE.

67

WOOD FLOORING

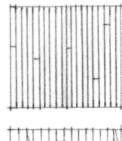

3" WIDE WOOD FLOORING
* DON'T FORGET WOOD COMES IN 8'-0"
  LENGTHS, SO ADD RANDOM END POINTS.

4" WOOD STRIPS WITH A LITTLE GRAIN
MEASURE 1'-0" INCREMENTS FIRST,
THEN DIVIDE INTO THIRDS. ALL IN H" PENCIL.
ADD RANDOM END POINTS & GRAIN.
GRAIN IS MORE STRAIGHT THAN CURVY.

4" WOOD STRIPS WITH A DOUBLE LINE
DRAW SAME AS 4" WOOD ABOVE WITH ONE
MORE LINE AND NO WOOD GRAIN.

4" WOOD STRIPS WITH A DOUBLE LINE
   AND SOME WOOD GRAIN
USE "H" PENCIL UNLESS YOU HAVE WHAT
I CALL A "HEAVY" HAND, THEN USE "2H" PENCIL.

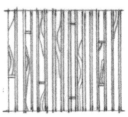

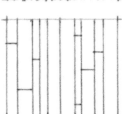

RANDOM WIDTHS AND LENGTHS
SIMPLE AND EASY!
USE WHEN YOU DON'T HAVE MUCH TIME.

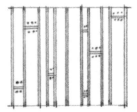

ADD DOUBLE LINES AND PEGS.
FUN AND A LITTLE MORE RUSTIC.

OLD WORLD WOOD FLOORING

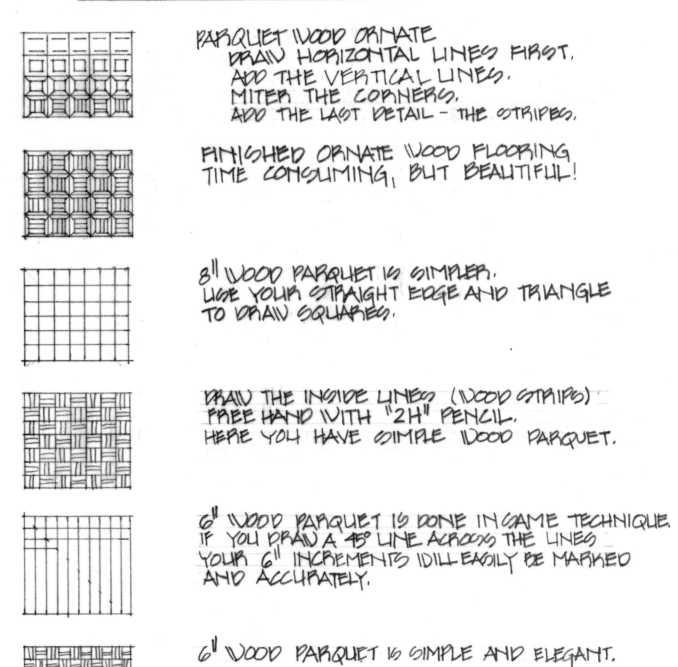

PARQUET WOOD ORNATE
  DRAW HORIZONTAL LINES FIRST.
  ADD THE VERTICAL LINES.
  MITER THE CORNERS.
  ADD THE LAST DETAIL - THE STRIPES.

FINISHED ORNATE WOOD FLOORING
TIME CONSUMING, BUT BEAUTIFUL!

8" WOOD PARQUET IS SIMPLER.
USE YOUR STRAIGHT EDGE AND TRIANGLE
TO DRAW SQUARES.

DRAW THE INSIDE LINES (WOOD STRIPS)
FREE HAND WITH "2H" PENCIL.
HERE YOU HAVE SIMPLE WOOD PARQUET.

6" WOOD PARQUET IS DONE IN SAME TECHNIQUE.
IF YOU DRAW A 45° LINE ACROSS THE LINES
YOUR 6" INCREMENTS WILL EASILY BE MARKED
AND ACCURATELY.

6" WOOD PARQUET IS SIMPLE AND ELEGANT.

MORE WOOD FLOORING

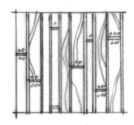

RANDOM WIDTHS AND LENGTHS
ADD WOOD GRAIN IN "2H" PENCIL.
KEEP IT SIMPLE - NOT TOO CURVY.

RANDOM WIDTHS CAN BE DRAWN FREEHAND.
START BY DRAFTING IN "2H" PENCIL
THEN DRAW FREEHAND IN "H" PENCIL.

8" BOARDS CAN BE DRAWN FREEHAND
SAME AS STYLE ABOVE.
ADD IN SIMPLE WOOD GRAIN IN "2H" PENCIL.

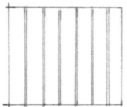

NOW...
   YOU FILL IN THE FREEHAND LINES.
   8" BOARDS

FREEHAND OVER THIS TO PRACTICE
RANDOM WIDTHS AND LENGTHS.

PRACTICE WOOD FLOORING OF YOUR CHOICE.
HAVE FUN!

FUN WOOD FLOORING

8" WOOD PARQUET
CAN BE DRAWN FREEFORM TO SHOW GRAIN.
NOTE ALL GRAIN LINES TOUCH BOTH SIDES.
"2H" PENCIL WORKS BEST.

6" WOOD PARQUET
DRAWN EXACTLY AS 8" ONLY SMALLER

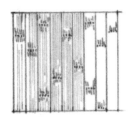

BAMBOO IN 6" STRIPS STARTS WITH DOTS
TO SHOW EDGES. A FEW SHORT STROKES
EXTEND FROM THE DOTS
THIN LINES IN "4H" PENCIL FORM THE GRAIN.

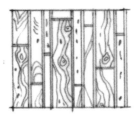

RECYCLED WOOD IS USUALLY RANDOM PLANKING.
KNOTS AND SCRATCH MARKS AND HOLES ARE
COMMON.
USE YOUR IMAGINATION OR COPY MINE.
"2H" PENCIL WORKS BEST.

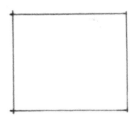

YOUR TURN...
DRAW THE FLOOR OF YOUR CHOICE.

71

CARPETING

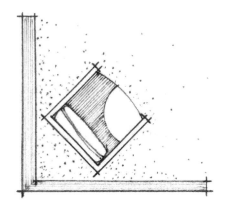

CARPET IS SHOWN BY A SERIES OF DOTS DRAWN WITH AN "F" PENCIL WITH MORE DOTS CLOSE TO THE WALLS AND FURNITURE.

DO NOT DRAW TAILS WITH YOUR DOTS.

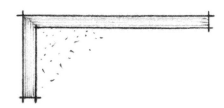

DOTS WITH TAILS LOOK <u>BAD</u>.

& DON'T DO CARPET LIKE THIS.

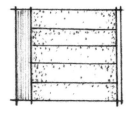

DEFINE STAIRS WITH DOTS TO SHOW DEPTH.

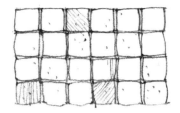

THE SAME DOTS CAN BE ADDED TO TILE TO CHANGE THE LOOK.

CHAPTER SIX

KITCHENS AND BATHS

itchens and bathrooms come in every size and design imaginable. The National Kitchen and Bath Association (NKBA) offers Kitchen Planning and Access Guidelines as well as Bathroom Planning and Access Guidelines online, at www.nkba.org. These comprehensive guides will tell you almost everything you need to know about the basics of layout and design in order to design your kitchen and bath.

Kitchens

There are many books available on kitchen design and layout; the kitchen is the hub of our home. My intention in this chapter is to show the three basic layouts used in kitchens over the last few years and the latest new triangle now used. I will illustrate the different layouts and elevations used in presentation drawings.

Baths

This chapter will show you almost everything you need to know in order to draw the details in your bath. Several basic layouts are shown and details of how to draw fixtures. Bathrooms can be as simple or complex as the designer chooses to make them. The drawings will follow this simplicity or the complexity. This chapter merely gives you the basis of possible layout spaces and details of how to draw the fixtures.

THE L-SHAPED KITCHEN

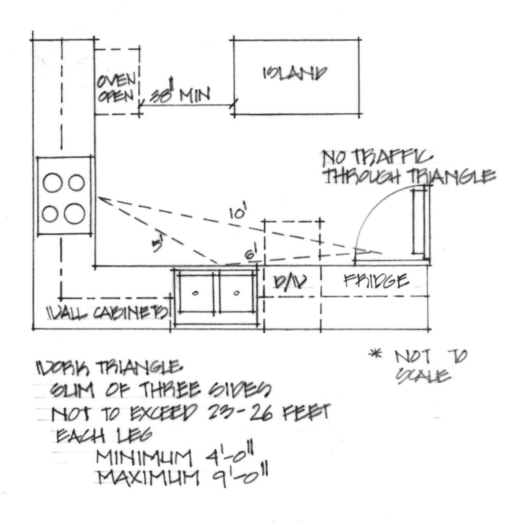

WORK TRIANGLE
SUM OF THREE SIDES
NOT TO EXCEED 23-26 FEET
EACH LEG
    MINIMUM 4'-0"
    MAXIMUM 9'-0"

CORRIDOR KITCHENS

TWO-PERSON CORRIDOR

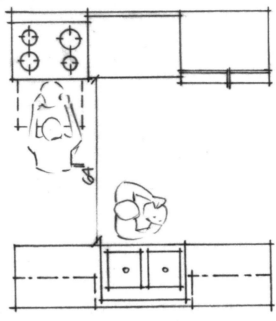

ONE-PERSON CORRIDOR

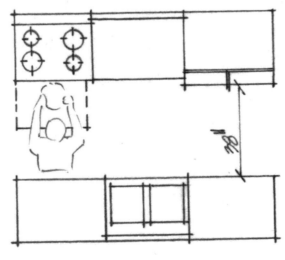

U-SHAPED KITCHEN

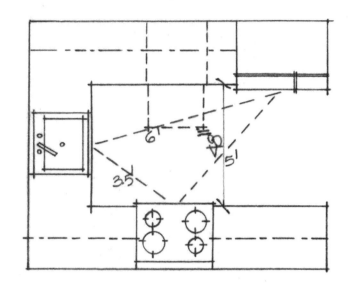

ONE-WALL KITCHEN

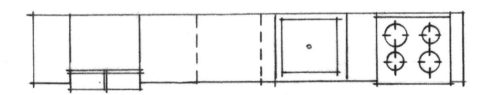

77

HEIGHT REQUIREMENTS

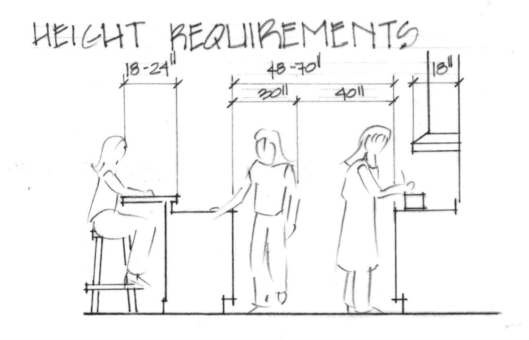

SPACE REQUIREMENTS

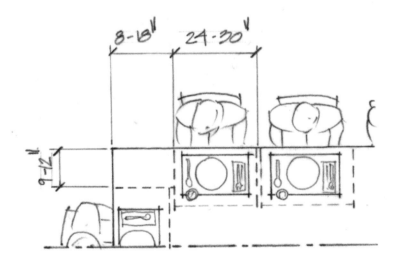

STANDARD SIZES

ITEM	WIDTH/LENGTH	HEIGHT	DEPTH	SPECIAL
KITCHEN COUNTER		36"	24-30"	28" WHEEL CHAIR
REFRIGERATOR	28-60"	5-6'	2'6"	
DISH WASHER	24"	24"	24"	
RANGE	30-36"	36"	24"	
OVEN	24-30"	24-30"	26"	
WASHER	30"	36"	30"	
DRYER	30"	36"	30"	
BATHROOM COUNTER	AS NEEDED	30-36"	24"	
TOILET	15'	28-30"	26"	
BATHTUB	5-7'-8"	16-24"	3-4'	
INTERIOR DOOR	2'6" -3'0"	6'8"	1 3/8"	
EXTERIOR DOOR	3'-0"	6'-8"	1 3/8"	
CEILING		8'-0"	8'-0"	

STANDARD HEIGHTS - CABINETS

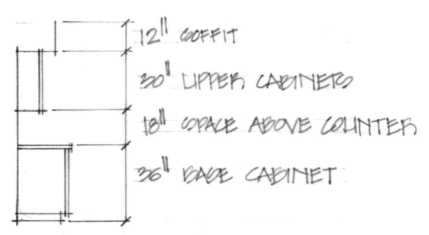

12" SOFFIT

30" UPPER CABINETS

18" SPACE ABOVE COUNTER

36" BASE CABINET

CUSTOM KITCHENS VARY WITH DESIGN, BUT THE BASICS REMAIN THE SAME. NOTE THE FOLLOWING
* 22" OPEN SPACE ABOVE THE SINK
30" OPEN SPACE ABOVE THE RANGE TOP

SWITCH SYMBOLS

SWITCH	NOTES
S	SINGLE SWITCH - TURNS ON ONE OR MORE LIGHTS FROM ONE LOCATION
S₃	3-WAY SWITCH - TURNS ON ONE OR MORE LIGHTS FROM TWO LOCATIONS. NEEDED FOR ROOMS WITH TWO ENTRIES
S₄	4-WAY SWITCH - IS USED TO TURN ON TWO 3-WAY SWITCHES WITH ONE OR MORE LIGHTS FROM THREE LOCATIONS
SSS	ONE LOCATION FOR THREE SWITCHES IN ONE GANG BOX
S DM	DIMMER SWITCH - USED TO CONTROL THE INTENSITY OF THE LIGHT
S₃DM	THREE WAY DIMMER SWITCH - USED TO CONTROL LIGHT INTENSITY FROM TWO LOCATIONS
SSS	THREE SWITCHES STACKED AT ONE LOCATION OFTEN USED FOR BATHROOM VENTILATION
S D	DOOR SWITCH - TURNS ON LIGHT WHEN DOOR IS OPENED PANTRY OR CLOSET USE
Ⓢ	CEILING PULL SWITCH - USED IN ATTICS OR CLOSETS
H T	THERMOSTAT - WALL-MOUNTED HEAT CONTROL

RECEPTACLE SYMBOLS

- HEIGHT - HEIGHT ABOVE FLOOR IF NOT STANDARD
- TYPE = TYPE OF RECEPTACLE

SINGLE RECEPTACLE - DEDICATED CIRCUIT

DOUBLE RECEPTACLE - STANDARD DUPLEX GROUNDED RECEPTACLE

QUADRUPLEX RECEPTACLE - TWO GANG BOX WITH FOUR RECEPTACLES

TRIPLEX RECEPTACLE - TWO GANG BOX WITH THREE RECEPTACLES

RECEPTACLE SYMBOLS CONTINUED

DUPLEX RECEPTACLE WITH SWITCH - TWO GANG BOX WITH A DUPLEX RECEPTACLE & A SWITCH

CLOCK RECEPTACLE - AREA IN CENTER IS RECESSED SO A CLOCK FIT FLUSH TO THE WALL

SPLIT-WIRED DUPLEX RECEPTACLE - TOP CONTROLLED BY A SWITCH. USED FOR LAMPS

WATERPROOF RECEPTACLE - COVERED

SINGLE FLOOR RECEPTACLE

DUPLEX FLOOR RECEPTACLE

GROUND FAULT INTERRUPTER - RECEPTACLE PROTECTED BY A GROUND FAULT CIRCUIT INTERRUPTER

RANGE RECEPTACLE - 50AMP - 4 WIRE

CLOTHES DRYER RECEPTACLE - 30 AMP - 4 WIRE

SINGLE RECEPTACLE WITH SWITCH

FLOOR JUNCTION BOX - CIRCUITS CONNECT IN BOX

BLANKED OUTLET - OUTLET NOT IN USE

JUNCTION BOX - CIRCUITS CONNECT IN BOX

LIGHTING SYMBOLS

CEILING-MOUNTED LIGHT - LABEL WITH TYPE
FL   FLUORESCENT LAMP
IN   INCANDESCENT LAMP
HA   HALOGEN LAMP

EXAMPLE:

IN

WALL-MOUNT FIXTURE

CEILING-MOUNTED WALL-WASHER FIXTURE

81

LIGHTING SYMBOLS CONTINUED

- RECESSED FIXTURE
- RECESSED FIXTURE ALTERNATIVE
- HANGING CEILING FIXTURE
- CEILING-MOUNTED SPOTLIGHT
- CEILING-MOUNTED LIGHT TRACK
- RECESSED FIXTURE - DAMP LOCATION - USED IN SHOWERS
- FLUORESCENT CEILING-MOUNTED FIXTURE
- FLUORESCENT LIGHT STRIP
- SURFACE-MOUNTED FLUORESCENT
- TRACK LIGHTING
- TELEPHONE
- DATA COMMUNICATIONS OUTLET
- TELEVISION OUTLET FOR CABLE
- DOOR BELL CHIME
- FAN HANGER OUTLET
- SMOKE DETECTOR - CEILING MOUNT
- WATER HEATER
- RADIANT HEAT - CEILING MOUNT

KITCHEN APPLIANCES

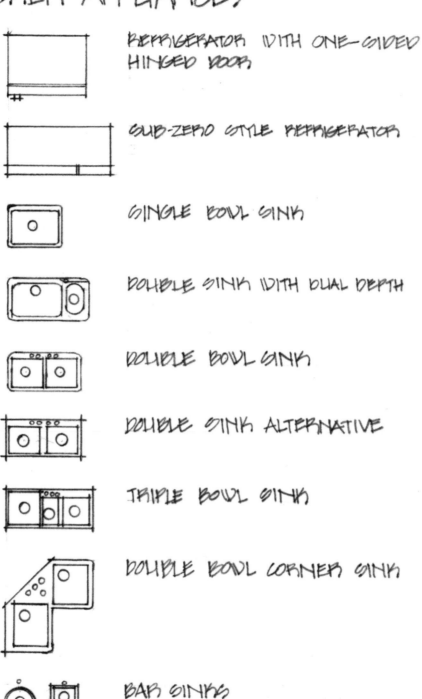

REFRIGERATOR WITH ONE-SIDED HINGED DOOR

SUB-ZERO STYLE REFRIGERATOR

SINGLE BOWL SINK

DOUBLE SINK WITH DUAL DEPTH

DOUBLE BOWL SINK

DOUBLE SINK ALTERNATIVE

TRIPLE BOWL SINK

DOUBLE BOWL CORNER SINK

BAR SINKS

KITCHEN APPLIANCES CONTINUED

 GAS COOKTOP

 GAS COOKTOP WITH CENTER DOWNDRAFT

 ELECTRIC RANGE WITH DOWN DRAFT

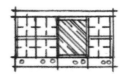 SIX-BURNER GAS COOKTOP WITH GRIDDLE

 GAS RANGE WITH DOOR HANDLE

 GRILL - DOWNDRAFT STYLE

 SINGLE COOK STATION - GAS

THERE ARE AS MANY COOKTOP
AND RANGE DESIGNS AS YOU CAN
IMAGINE AND DRAW.

TYPICAL KITCHEN REFLECTED CEILING

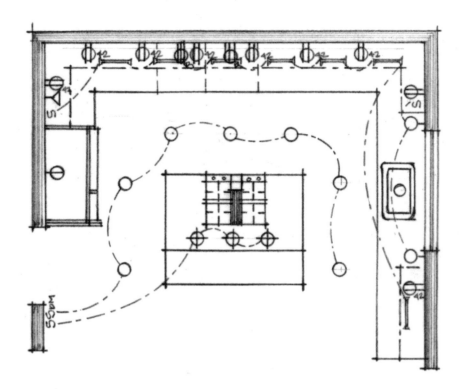

SCHEDULE

⊕ₙ	RANGE RECEPTACLE
⊕	DUPLEX RECEPTACLE
⊖	SINGLE RECEPTACLE
⊙	WALL-MOUNT LIGHT FIXTURE
⊕	CEILING FIXTURE - HANGING
⊙	RECESSED FIXTURE
◁	TELEPHONE
⊢⊣	UNDER-COUNTER FLUORESCENT STRIP
S	SINGLE SWITCH
Sᴅᴍ	SWITCH WITH DIMMER

KITCHEN ELEVATIONS

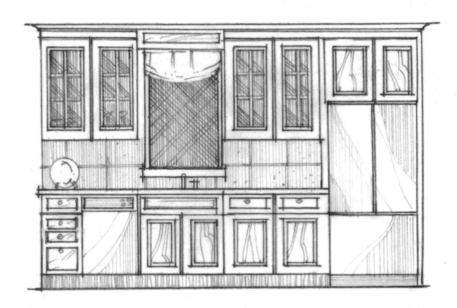

KITCHEN ELEVATIONS ARE USED TO SHOW DESIGN DETAILS, THE CABINET STYLE AND DESIGN STYLE OF THE AREA.

KITCHEN ELEVATIONS ARE GENERALLY IN HALF-INCH SCALE IN ORDER TO SHOW MORE DETAIL.

YOU CAN SHOW DETAILS OF THE FOLLOWING:
- WINDOWS
- WINDOW COVERINGS
- CABINET STYLE
- BACK-SPLASH DESIGN
- MOLDING
- SPECIAL EFFECTS

BASIC BATH LAYOUTS

BASIC BATH LAYOUTS CONTINUED

BATHROOMS

TOILETS CAN BE DRAWN WITH A TEMPLATE BUT LOOK MUCH BETTER DRAWN ARTISTICALLY.

TEMPLATES

TOILETS DRAWN WITHOUT TEMPLATES

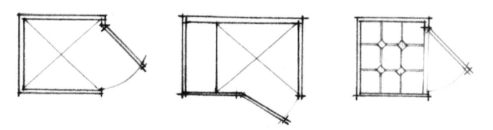

SHOWERS CAN BE SIMPLY DRAWN OR DRAWN WITH MORE DETAIL TO SHOW TILE DESIGN.

BATHTUBS NEED TO BE DRAWN WITH MORE THAN A SINGLE LINE.

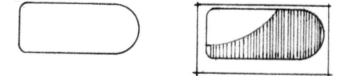

ADD SHADOWS

MORE TUB & SHOWER TECHNIQUES

TUB ENCLOSURE WITH SHOWER CURTAIN

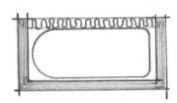

TUB ENCLOSURE WITH SLIDING DOORS

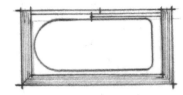

TUB ENCLOSURE WITH FRONT EXTENSION

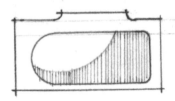

CORNER SHOWER

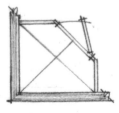

WALK-IN SHOWER

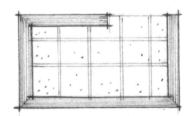

CHAPTER Seven

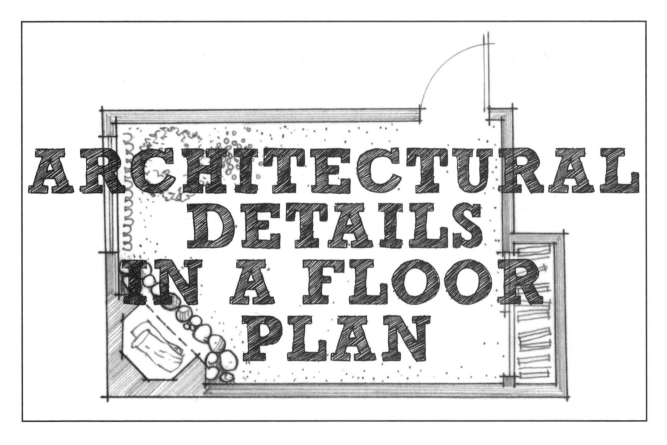

ARCHITECTURAL
DETAILS
IN A FLOOR
PLAN

It is all in the details. Add clothing in a closet, put a few logs in the fire-place, add draperies to the windows and your drawing will have a personality of its own. The architectural details in a floor plan can make the difference between an ordinary drawing and an exquisite drawing.

In this chapter I will illustrate some of the details that can make that difference. If you draw your details simply and precisely, it will not take much more time to execute your drawing and it will look ten times better. Add a few perfectly placed plants and you have a small work of art!

ARCHITECTURAL DETAILS

PLACING CLOTHING IN A CLOSET ADDS LIFE TO YOUR DRAWING. IT CAN BE DRAWN FREEHAND OR USING A TRIANGLE.

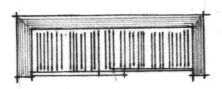

USING A TRIANGLE IS SIMPLE AND GIVES YOU A MORE CONTEMPORARY LOOK.

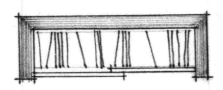

CLOTHES CAN BE DRAWN IN A SIMPLE MANNER IN A FREEHAND FORM.

DRAPERIES CAN BE SHOWN IN SEVERAL WAYS. USING GUIDELINES AND A CONNECTED U MAKE A REALISTIC LOOK.

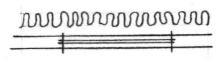

WIGGLY LINES DRAWN BETWEEN GUIDELINES

* NOTE: ALWAYS LEAVE 6" BETWEEN THE WINDOW & THE WALL.

ARCHITECTURAL DETAILS CONTINUED

 VERTICAL BLINDS ARE DRAWN WITH ANGLED LINES.

 VERTICAL BLINDS CAN BE DRAWN WITH A DOUBLE LINE.

 OR IN A VERY SIMPLE ANGLE.

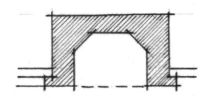 FIRE PLACES LOOK BEST FILLED WITH A 45-DEGREE LINE.

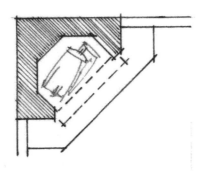 CORNER FIREPLACE WITH LOGS

 FIREPLACE WITH RIVER ROCK HEARTH

NOTE: THE FRONT OF THE RIVER ROCK IS DRAWN UNEVENLY JUST LIKE ROCK.

AREA RUGS

AREA RUGS ADD YOUR PERSONAL STYLE TO A FLOOR PLAN. THE SOURCES FOR AREA RUG DESIGN IDEAS ARE INFINITE. THE INTERNET IS A WONDERFUL SOURCE FOR INSPIRATION. THERE ARE SOME SIMPLE GUIDELINES FOR SUCCESSFUL FULL-LOOKING RUGS.

PICK A STANDARD SIZE THAT FITS THE ROOM.

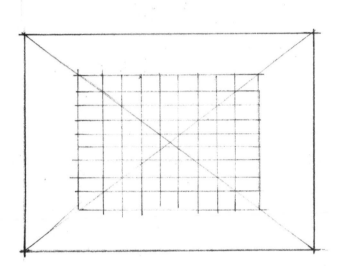

9'-0" x 12'-0"
SKETCH YOUR DESIGN WITH GUIDELINES.

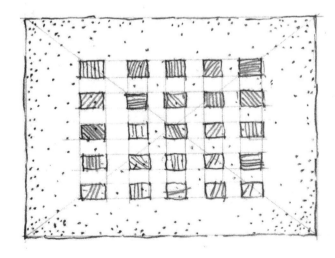

TRACE OVER WITH FREEHAND USING VARIABLE PRESSURE & BROKEN LINE WEIGHT. FILL IN TO MAKE MORE APPEALING DOT LIKE CARPET.

AREA RUG IDEAS

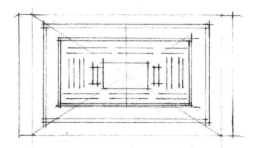

LAYOUT A DETAILED RUG.
ADD A FRINGE ON THE
ENDS FOR INTEREST.

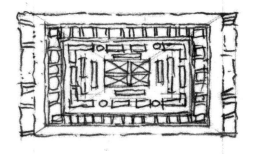

ADD DETAIL WITH
FREEHAND.
ADD FRINGE DETAIL.

CAREFULLY RENDER
ALL DETAILED AREAS.
ADD DOTS.

SIMPLER AREA RUGS

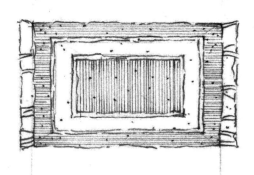

SIMPLE DESIGNS CAN
MAKE A BIG IMPACT.

SOME FUN AREA RUGS

PLANTS

PLANTS ADD PERSONALITY TO ANY DRAWING.
START WITH A CIRCLE FOR INDIVIDUAL PLANTS.
CLUSTER PLANTS TOGETHER.

DRAW THE CIRCLE.

 DRAW STRAIGHT LINES WITH TRIANGLE.

 OR DRAW FREEHAND.

 OUTSIDE BORDER LINES FREEHAND
WITH TWO CIRCLES. I LEFT IT PARTLY
UNFINISHED TO SHOW TECHNIQUE.

SQUIGGLE OR FERN STYLE IS SHOWN
IN TWO STEPS. DRAW THE ARMS.
ADD SQUIGGLY LINES TO FORM
PLANTS. SIMPLE & ATTRACTIVE.

SIMPLE & LOOSE. EASY TO DRAW.
JUST DRAWN LOOSELY ON THE PERIMETER.

MORE PLANT DESIGNS

 LEAF-SHAPED PLANT

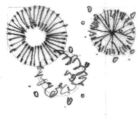 SMALL IRREGULAR CIRCLES FORM AN INTERESTING LOOK.

 INDIVIDUAL LEAVES

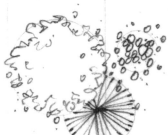 CLUSTER PLANTS IN GROUPS. BE SURE TO OVERLAP.

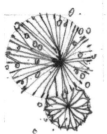 ADD A LITTLE VARIETY TO THE PLANTS IN CLUSTERS.

OR JUST DRAW TWO PLANTS.

PLANT VARIATIONS

 ALWAYS START WITH A CIRCLE AND ADD DIFFERENT FINISH STYLES.

 QUICKLY DRAW A PERIMETER.

OR

 ADD INTERIOR ELEMENTS.

OR

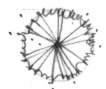 COMBINE SEVERAL STYLES.

 DRAW LARGER TO REPRESENT A TREE.

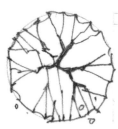 SIMPLIFY THE DRAWING.

MORE PLANT VARIATIONS

EXTEND THE SIMPLE & LOOSE STYLE TO THE INTERIOR OF THE CIRCLE.

ADD CIRCLES TO SOFTEN THE EDGES.

EXTEND THE WIGGLY LINES TO LOOK LIKE BRANCHES.

ADD A PLANTER BOX.

OR ADD A POT.

ADD CIRCLES TO FERN DESIGN.

AND MORE

 ADD CIRCLES TO STRAIGHT LINES.

 ADD CURVED BRANCHES.

 COMBINE CURVED BRANCHES WITH CIRCLES.

 ADD A DEFINED PERIMETER.

 BE CREATIVE.

BE CAREFUL NOT TO MAKE MISTAKES.

TOO LARGE   TOO SMALL   TO SPARSE

LEAVES TOO BIG FOR SCALE

CHAPTER eight

INTERIOR ELEVATIONS

single interior can have a million different looks. Designers draw elevations in order to show the details they want to use in their interiors. Elevations are an easy way to show your client exactly how you see the interior, wall by wall. Your design ideas become very clear with good elevations.

Your elevations can show how the window coverings are to be designed, or how the fireplace is to look, or even what style the cabinets should be. In addition, elevations show placement of windows and doors, art and mirrors. Elevations allow you to show your client many effects in a more detailed manner. Anything that is placed in the interior can be shown in elevations.

Your elevations can be drawn in ½-inch scale and then copied in a smaller size. This makes the details that you have drawn look much more precise.

This chapter begins by showing how to draw your elevations.

DRAWING ELEVATIONS

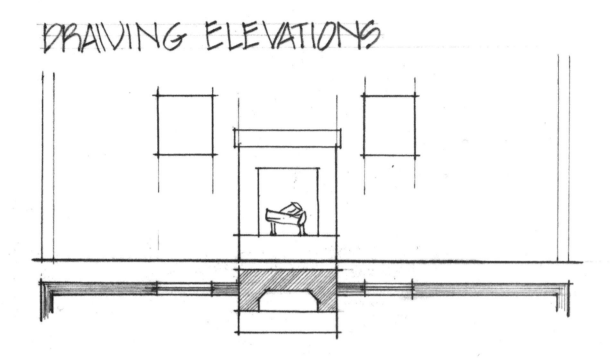

THE ELEVATIONS ARE LAID OUT BY DRAWING LINES
EXTENDING FROM WALL YOU PLAN TO DRAW.
DRAW THE LINES AS IF YOU WERE STANDING IN
FRONT OF THE WALL LOOKING AT IT.

LAY OUT THE WALL ELEVATION IN ¼" SCALE FIRST
TO SEE IF THE PROPORTIONS WORK WELL, THEN
REDRAW IN ½" SCALE TO SHOW MORE DETAIL.

MY ILLUSTRATIONS ARE ALL IN ¼" SCALE
AND ARE TO GIVE YOU IDEAS ONLY.

FURNITURE IN ELEVATION

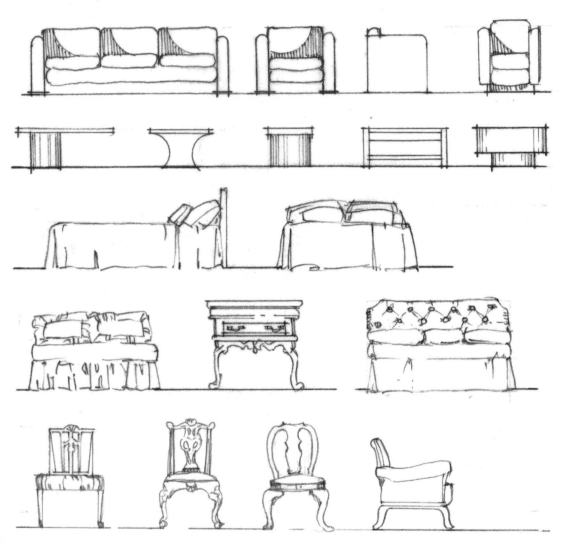

FURNITURE IN THE ELEVATION IS SIMPLIFIED WITH
ENOUGH DETAIL TO KEEP IT INTERESTING, BUT THE
BACKGROUND IS WHERE THE EMPHASIS OF THE
DRAWING NEEDS TO BE TO SHOW ARCHITECTURAL
DETAILS.

DRAWING WINDOWS

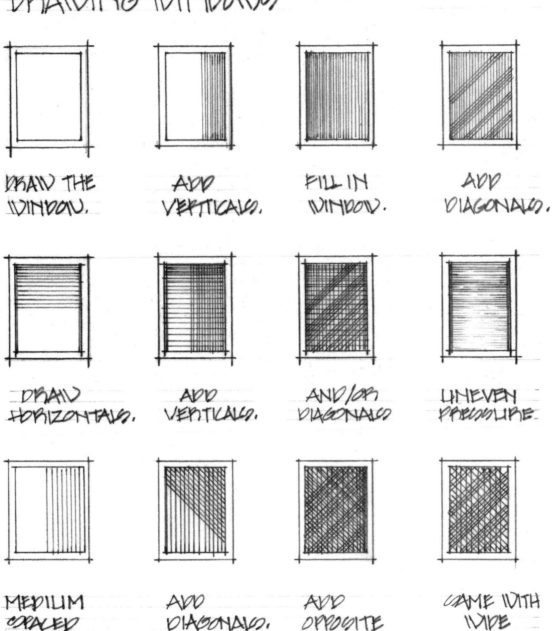

DRAW THE
WINDOW.

ADD
VERTICALS.

FILL IN
WINDOW.

ADD
DIAGONALS.

DRAW
HORIZONTALS.

ADD
VERTICALS.

AND/OR
DIAGONALS

UNEVEN
PRESSURE

MEDIUM
SPACED
VERTICALS

ADD
DIAGONALS.

ADD
OPPOSITE
DIAGONAL.

SAME WITH
WIDE
SPACING

107

WINDOWS

  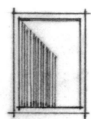 

HATCH TECHNIQUE	2H HATCH H SHADOW	H SHADOW LINED	FREEHAND CROSSHATCH

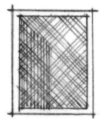  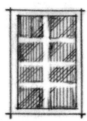 

DIAGONALS WITH SHADOW	MULLIONS FREEHAND	MULLIONS DIAGONAL	VARIETY

DRAPERIES OUTSIDE VIEW

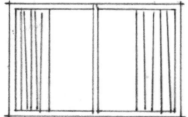 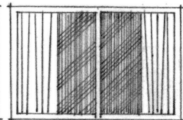 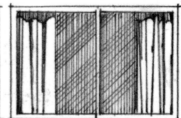

MORE WINDOWS LOOKING OUT

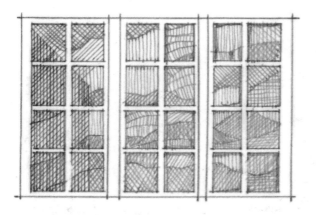 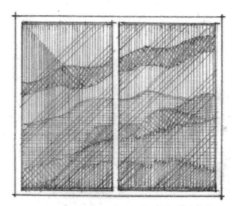

SAME VIEW ~ DIFFERENT WINDOWS

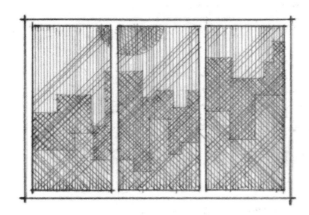 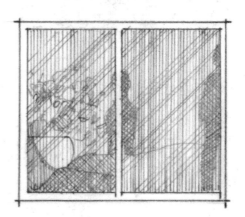

CITY SCAPES

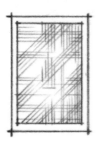 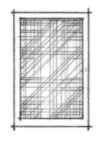 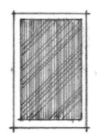 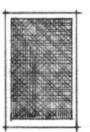

SIMPLE   A LITTLE MORE   AND MORE   AND...

109

WINDOW COVERINGS

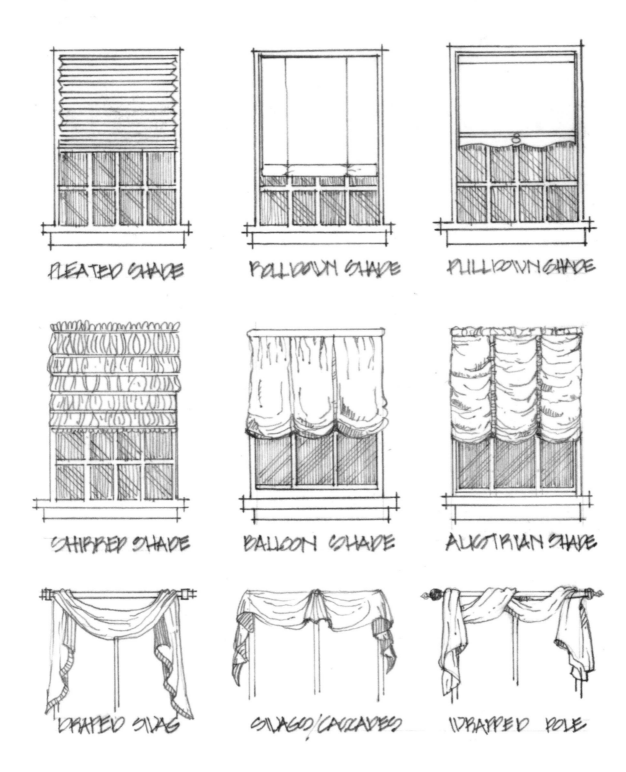

PLEATED SHADE   ROLLDOWN SHADE   PULLDOWN SHADE

SHIRRED SHADE   BALLOON SHADE   AUSTRIAN SHADE

DRAPED SWAG   SWAGS/CASCADES   WRAPPED POLE

MORE WINDOW COVERINGS

 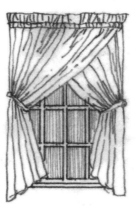 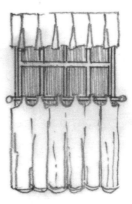

TRADITIONAL
SWAG

PRISCILLA
CURTAINS

CAFÉ
CURTAINS

PINCH PLEAT DRAPERIES OVER ROLLER SHADES

DRAPERIES

GEORGIAN TIEBACK

FRENCH PLEAT

CORNICE/HOLDBACK

OVER DRAPERY VALANCE

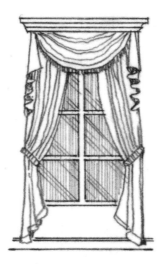

WOOD CORNICE SWAGS/CASCADES

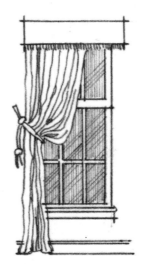

ASYMMETRIC TIE-BACK/CORNICE BOX

ONE WALL, DIFFERENT STYLES

AND MORE STYLES

CHAPTER nine

EXTERIOR ELEVATIONS

Designers seldom draw exterior elevations; generally they are left to the architect to draw when designing the exterior of homes or other buildings. However, I have assisted with the exterior design of many homes and gardens and have included a chapter on exterior elevations for interior designers because you never know when a remodel or addition that you are requested to do might include exterior design to go along with the interior design. It never ceases to amaze me what people will ask you to do. Each designer must decide how much she or he is willing to contribute at any given time for any given project. If you have the talent, why not extend your capabilities to overall design.

As with interior elevations, exterior elevations can be drawn in ½-inch scale and then copied in a smaller size. This will make the details that you have drawn look much more precise.

EXTERIOR ELEVATIONS

INTERIOR DESIGNERS INFREQUENTLY DRAW EXTERIOR ELEVATIONS. I ADDED A SHORT CHAPTER WITH TECHNIQUES THAT YOU CAN APPLY TO INTERIOR AND EXTERIOR DRAWINGS. AT SOME TIME YOU MAY DECIDE TO USE YOUR DRAWING SKILLS TO DESIGN A TOTAL HOME CONCEPT, INCLUDING EXTERIOR ELEVATIONS. I HAVE PERSONALLY DESIGNED THREE OF MY OWN PERSONAL HOMES, INCLUDING THE DESIGN OF THE EXTERIOR. ONE OF MY DESIGNER FRIENDS DREW EXTERIOR ELEVATIONS FOR REAL ESTATE COMPANIES FOR SEVERAL YEARS.

EXTERIOR ELEVATION

AN EXTERIOR ELEVATION IS QUITE BLAND WHEN
DRAWN WITHOUT APPROPRIATE DETAIL.

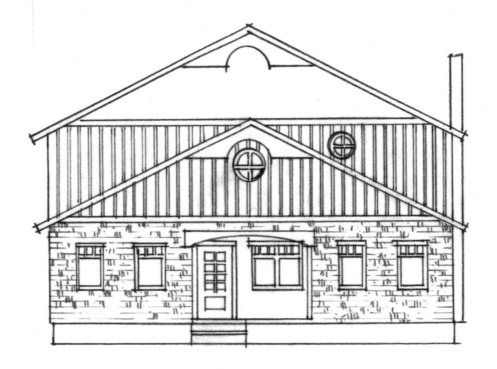

COMPARE THIS DRAWING TO THE ONE ON
THE PREVIOUS PAGE. WHICH IS ALIVE?

EXTERIOR SIDING

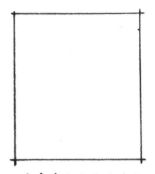

MEASURE BOARD WIDTH AND MAKE A DOT BELOW THE AREA TO BE RENDERED. THIS WAY YOU CAN ERASE IT LATER.

DRAW BOARD LINES IN "H" PENCIL IN SINGLE LINES. SELECT A SIDING WIDTH AND DRAW IT CONSISTENTLY.

WOODGRAIN IS DRAWN IN H OR 2H PENCIL. VARY THE LINE WEIGHT AND DIRECTION OF THE GRAIN AS YOU DRAW IT. ALSO VARY THE AMOUNT OF GRAIN LINES THROUGH THE DRAWING.

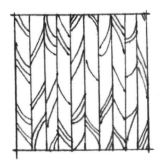

<u>DON'T</u> DRAW THE WOOD GRAIN IN A CONTRIVED MANNER AS IT WILL LOOK FAKE.

SIDING

FISHSCALE SHINGLES: USE AN 8"
GRID AND ALTERNATE ROWS.
NOTE SHADOW ON SOME SHINGLES.
ADD SHADOW WITH CURVED LINES.

FREEHAND DOUBLE LINE BRICKS.
DRAW GUIDELINES FIRST IN 4H.
REDRAW IN H PENCIL.

PLAIN ROUGH SAWN SIDING
WITH BATTS IS SIMPLY DRAWN.
USE 2H TO DRAW GRAIN.

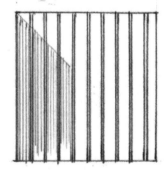

VERTICAL SIDING CAN BE DRAWN
WITH NO GRAIN AND A DOUBLE
LINE.

SIDING SHADOWS

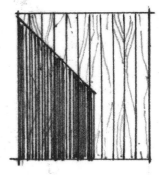

DRAW THE WALL SIDING WITHOUT SHADOWS. DECIDE ON SHADOW AREAS AND DRAW VERTICAL LINES USING F PENCIL.

DON'T DRAW THE SHADOW LINES FAR APART. IT IS TOO CONFUSING.

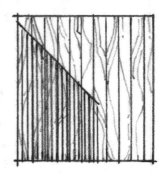

DRAW HORIZONTAL GUIDELINES SPACED APPROXIMATELY 8" APART TO DRAW SHINGLES.

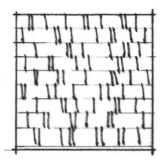

RANDOMLY DRAW FREE HAND LINES. VARY BETWEEN ONE AND TWO LINES PLACED SIDE BY SIDE. USE AN H OR 2H PENCIL.

SIDING (CONTINUED)

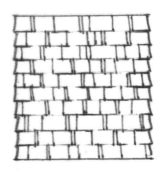

ADD A VARIETY OF PENCIL LINES TO MAKE SHINGLES LOOK MORE AUTHENTIC.

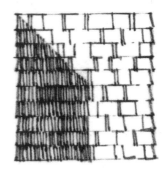

SHADOW LINES SHOULD BE HAND DRAWN ONE ROW AT A TIME. USE A H OR 2H PENCIL. CHANGE THE PRESSURE TO CREATE THE LOOK OF LIGHT.

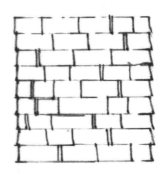

DON'T DRAW THE SHINGLES TOO UNIFORM AS THEY WILL LOOK MORE LIKE BLOCKS OR BRICKS.

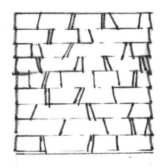

DON'T PUT VERTICALS AT AN ANGLE. IT DOES NOT LOOK REALISTIC.

SIDING CONTINUED

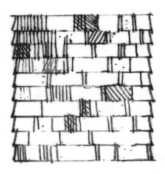

SHINGLES CAN BE MADE MORE INTERESTING WITH INTERESTING SHADING AND VARIETY IN YOUR STROKES. ADD A FEW DOTS FOR MORE TEXTURE.

ROCK WALLS CAN LOOK GREAT IF DRAWN WITH SUFFICIENT DETAIL. NOTE THE NATURAL ROCK SHAPE WITH NOT MUCH SPACE BETWEEN SHAPES. VARY THE SHADING DESIGN AND PATTERN LIGHT AND DARK.

DON'T DRAW UNREALISTIC ROCK/STONE SHAPES. THE EDGE WOULD NOT BE A STRAIGHT LINE, AS SHOWN HERE.

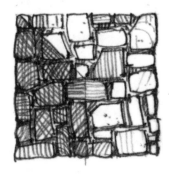

SHADOW CAN BE ADDED BY ADDING MORE TEXTURE. THE SPACE BETWEEN THE STONE IS DARKENED TO SHOW DEPTH. JUST A FEW ADDITIONAL LINES CAN MAKE A HUGE DIFFERENCE.

SIDING CONTINUED

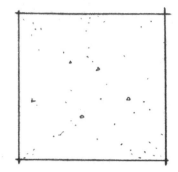

STUCCO LOOKS BEST WHEN DOTS AND MARKS ARE VARIED.

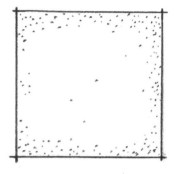

__DON'T__ DOT OR STIPPLE AROUND THE EDGES CREATING A BORDER BLEND INTO THE CENTER. DOT LESS.

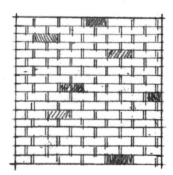

BRICK LOOKS GOOD RENDERED OR NOT.

STACK STONE AKA SLUMP STONE IS TOTALLY DRAWN BY HAND. IT IS A POPULAR LOOK.

SIDING CONTINUED

FLUTED CONCRETE BLOCK IS DRAWN WITH VERTICAL GUIDELINES FIRST. FREEHAND LINES WITH VARIED AND BROKEN PRESSURE ARE ADDED. ADD DOTS (STIPPLE) FOR INTEREST.

SHAKES ARE SIMILAR TO THE BASIC SHINGLE TECHNIQUE WITH MORE DOUBLE VERTICALS.

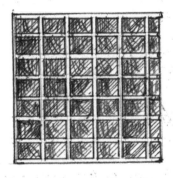

GLASS BLOCKS CAN BE USED ON AN EXTERIOR WALL.

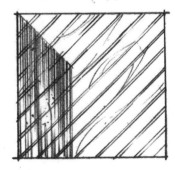

DIAGONAL SIDING IS USED FOR ACCENT OCCASIONALLY. NOTE THE SHADOW IS VERTICAL.

SIDING CONTINUED

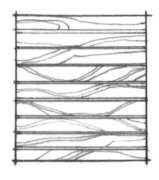

HORIZONTAL SIDING CAN BE DRAWN USING YOUR T-SQUARE AND ADDING GRAIN FREEHAND.

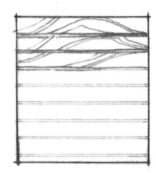

OR DRAW GUIDELINES AND FILL IN DRAWING FREEHAND.

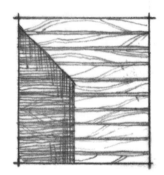

DRAW THE SHADOW FREEHAND USING MOSTLY HORIZONTAL LINES.

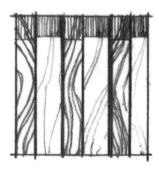

BOARD ON BOARD VS. BOARD AND BATT CAN BE DRAWN BY DEFINING THE OUTER BOARDS. USE H PENCIL FOR OUTSIDE PLANKS AND 2H PENCIL FOR BACKGROUND.

SIDING OPTIONS

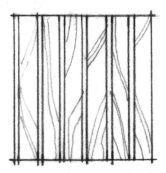

BOARD AND BATT DRAWN SIMPLY.

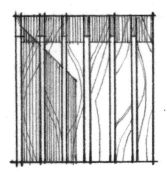

ADDING SHADOW DEFINES THE LOOK AND MAKES THE LOOK MORE DRAMATIC.

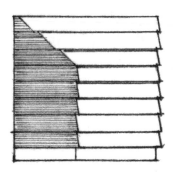

SHIPLAP SIDING IS DENOTED BY THE EDGE OF THE BOARD AND THE EDGE OF THE SHADOW.

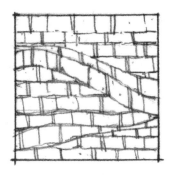

FREEFORM SHINGLES ADD A LITTLE CHARACTER TO SOME DESIGNS. CAN ADD SHADOWS.

ROOF DETAILS

ROOF SHINGLES ARE BASICALLY DRAWN THE SAME AS SIDEWALL SHINGLES. DRAW GUIDELINES 4" APART.

SPACE VERTICAL LINES IN A RANDOM MANNER USING YOUR "H" PENCIL.

ADD SHINGLE CAP LINE AT TOP. EDGE THE SIDES TO SHOW PROFILE. ADD SHADOW AT BOTTOM.

SIDE VIEW WITH RIDGE CAP ON UPPERMOST EDGE

ROOF DETAILS CONTINUED

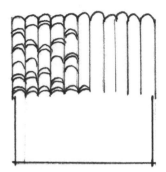

TILE ROOFS BEGIN WITH VERTICAL GUIDELINES 6" APART. DRAW THE ARCS AT RANDOM ON EACH ROW

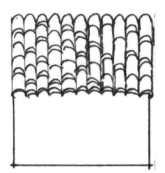

DRAW LINES BETWEEN THE ROWS OF THE ARCS USING "H" OR "F" PENCIL IN A VARIED MANNER.

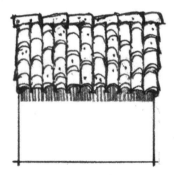

COMPLETE THE ROWS OF TILE BY ADDING RIDGE CAP. ADD DOTS (AKA STIPPLE) FOR ADDED PERSONALITY. ADD LINES FOR A SHADOW ALONG THE BOTTOM.

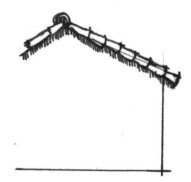

SIDE VIEW OF TILE ROOF

ROOF VARIATIONS

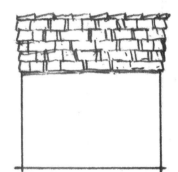

BASIC SHINGLE CAN HAVE MORE PIZAZZ WITH THE ADDITION OF MORE VERTICAL LINES.

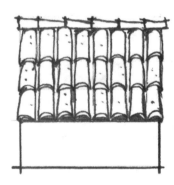

SHINGLES CAN BE DRAWN FREEHAND FOR MORE CASUAL LOOK.

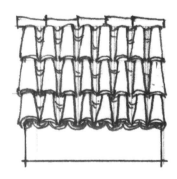

TILE ROOF CAN BE DRAWN IN A MORE PRECISE MANNER BY DRAWING VERTICAL AND HORIZONTAL GUIDELINES.

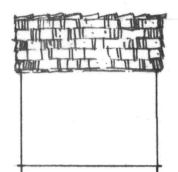

TILE ROOF CAN BE DRAWN WITH THE SAME GUIDELINES, BUT FLARING THE TILES AT THE BOTTOM OF EACH TILE.

MORE ROOF IDEAS

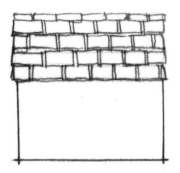

SHINGLES CAN BE DRAWN WITH REGULAR SPACING AND A DOUBLE LINE IN AN EVEN MANNER.

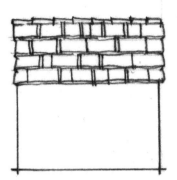

YOU CAN DRAW SHINGLES IN A MORE RANDOM MANNER.

SIDE VIEW OF SHINGLE ROOF WITH FASCIA BOARD

EXTERIOR TREES

EXTERIOR TREES CAN BE DRAWN IN A WIDE
VARIETY OF STYLES. SEVERAL ARE SHOWN
ON THE FOLLOWING PAGES.

TREES CONTINUED

TREES CONTINUED

WITH ROCKS
AND WATER

TREES CONTINUED

TREES IN FRONT

ADDING DETAILS TAKES A DRAWING
FROM ORDINARY
TO
BEAUTIFUL!!

CHAPTER ten

SECTIONS

Sections cut right through a building, an orthographic projection as if cut down the middle by a knife. A section opens the space to show the relevant architectural and structural information in architecture. In interior design, the section is used to show the relationships of rooms. Everything can more easily be shown in elevations, however, so a residential designer seldom will have the need to draw a section. Drawing sections are included in this book simply because when we have several floors in a building it is imperative to understand stairways, window alignment, and the use of spaces in a home. When designing or redesigning an interior space, designers need always to be aware of what is above and below the space. Sections are a great way to think it through on paper, and not make a mistake on design. For instance, you would not want a cinema room with surround sound below a nursery or even a master bedroom.

Sections and elevations are both vertical drawings; they retain the true proportions, actual scale, and same shape, but elevations show one wall of one room at a time. The relationships between the floors, walls, and roof are shown in section drawings. Door locations, window locations, as well as heights, cabinetry, stair locations are also shown.

If you were to draw an architectural section, you would want to show the following:

- Type of foundation
- Floor system
- Wall construction, interior and exterior
- Beam or column sizes and materials
- Wall heights
- Elevation of floors

- Floor members
- Floor sheathing
- Ceiling members
- Roof pitch
- Roof sheathing
- Insulation
- Roof finish material

It is always good to also add a human figure to the drawing to help illustrate the scale of the spaces.

The section generally is drawn in ¼-inch scale by interior designers to show how the rooms relate one to another. This chapter includes illustrations of simple section. Because this book is focused on design presentation drawing and drafting, and is not a book for architects, only a simple description and simple diagrams are included. More detailed drawings of sections with construction details can be found in architectural books.

BUILDING SECTION

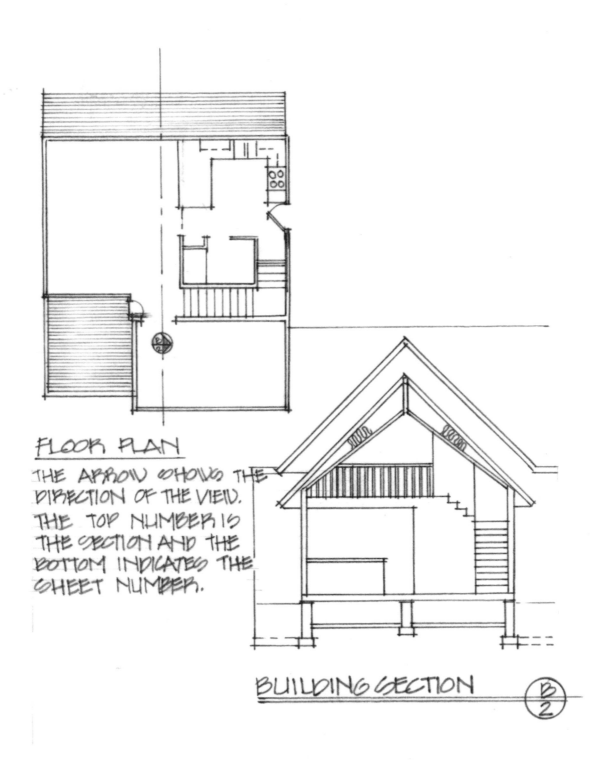

FLOOR PLAN

THE ARROW SHOWS THE
DIRECTION OF THE VIEW.
THE TOP NUMBER IS
THE SECTION AND THE
BOTTOM INDICATES THE
SHEET NUMBER.

BUILDING SECTION

$\dfrac{B}{2}$

139

DEFINITION BY LINE WEIGHT

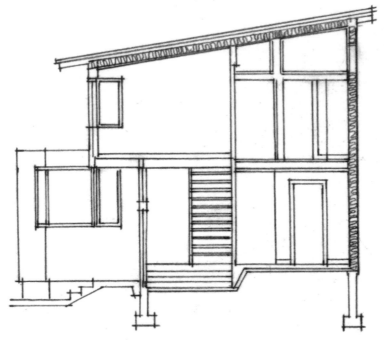

NOTE HOW THE USE OF LINE WEIGHTS SUGGESTS
THE SENSE OF DEPTH.

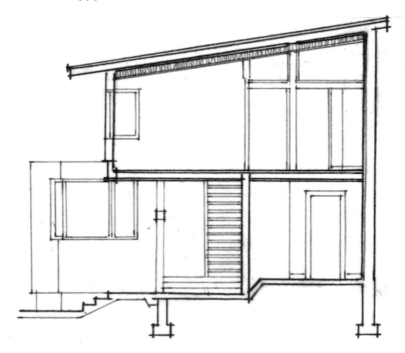

GLOSSARY

Accordion Doors   Folding doors with narrow vertical panels that stack side by side.

Alcove   Indented opening off a wall, sometimes used for displaying art.

Anthropometrics   The comparison and study of human body measurements.

Apron   Horizontal trim under the sill of the interior window.

Architect   A professional who designs three-dimensional space and creates the floor plans, interior and exterior design.

Architectural Elements   The floors, ceilings, windows, doors, fireplaces, walls, cabinetry, and other fixtures or details that are built in an interior.

Area Rugs   Type of rug that can define an area for conversation.

ASID   American Society of Interior Design.

Attic   Space between the ceiling and the roof.

Awning Window   Top hinging window that opens out.

Axonometric Drawing   Type of drawing that includes isometric, elevation, oblique, and plan oblique drawings; a single-view drawing with all lines parallel and projected at an angle. Also referred to as paraline drawing.

Background   Components of a drawing that take place in the space behind the center of interest.

Backsplash   Area behind a countertop, usually measuring 4" to 18" vertically.

Balcony   Deck above ground level, projecting from the interior or exterior.

Baluster   Small vertical component in the railing used between the top rail and the stair treads or bottom rail.

Balustrade   The railing formed by the newel post, baluster, and handrail.

Bannister   Handrail with supporting posts used beside a stairway.

Barrier-free Design   Design approach with no physical obstacles or barriers, allowing free movement in the environment.

Base Cabinets   The lower segment of cabinets in kitchens or other rooms that support the countertops.

Baseboard   The finishing board of a variety of different materials that covers the area where the wall joins the floor.

Batten   Strip of wood or metal used to cover vertical joints between boards.

Bay Window   A window projecting away from the exterior of the building.

Beadboard   Wood paneling with vertical grooves milled so it looks like board and batten walls.

Beam   Horizontal structural member supporting a load.

Bearing Wall   A wall that supports a structural floor or roof load.

Bifold Door   Doors fold together to open.

Black-line Print   A type of reproduction of drawings that has black lines on a gray background.

Blueprints   Floor plans printed in blue ink used for the construction of buildings.

Board and Batten   Siding technique that uses narrow strips of wood, called battens, placed evenly in a pattern over the wooden siding; a technique originally designed to hide the vertical cracks between the boards.

Breast   The front of the fireplace and chimney.

Brown-line Print   Same as a black-line print, but the lines are brown; also known as a sepia print.

Bubble Diagram   The first step of programming where bubbles represent zones and areas where the spaces will be designed in proximity to one another.

Building Code   Federal, state, or local ruling laws that stipulate building safety and health requirements to help ensure the safety, health, and welfare of the general public during construction and occupancy.

Bullnose   180-degree rounding of the edge of a material, usually on wood or stone. *See also* Nosing.

Cabinetry   Fine finished woodworking.

CAD/CADD   Computer-aided drawing/computer-aided drafting and design.

Capital   The decorative top of a pillar or column.

Casement   A window frame that is hinged on the side.

Casement Window   A hinged window that opens outward.

Casing   Trim surrounding window and door openings.

Cathedral Window   An angular window set in the gable of a room with a slanted ceiling.

Chair Rail   A trim piece or molding attached to the wall at chair-back height, generally placed to protect the wall from damage from the back of the chair.

Chandelier   A decorative, ceiling-mounted luminaire, usually with several arms or branches for candles or lamps.

Clerestory Window   Window positioned near the top of a wall.

Column   Vertical structural or non-structural member.

Combination Window   A window with one section of stationary glass and the other a different type of window, like an awning.

Compass   Drafting instrument used to draw circles or curves.

Concrete   Mixture of gravel, sand, cement, and water.

Construction Drawings   *See* Working Drawings.

Corbel   Masonry or woodworking that is stepped out to protect the wall.

Cross-hatching   A drawing technique used to create visual texture, using pencil or pen, superimposing the crossing of lines in opposite lines, usually X's done many times; this technique often is used in the poché of walls in a floor plan.

Crown Molding   Molding used where the ceiling meets the wall.

Demolition Plan   A drawing drafted to show elements of a project that are to be eliminated.

Design Concept   A design or an idea for a design to find the solution to a problem, pulling together different ideas to form a viable design.

Detail Drawing   Scale drawing that describes in detail a specific feature of a design concept.

Dimensions   Numerical values used to indicate size and distance in a drawing.

Door Jamb   The vertical elements that form the inside of a door opening held together by a horizontal member.

Door Stop   An object or device used to hold a door open or closed, or to prevent a door from opening too widely.

Double Action Door   Door that swings both inward and outward.

Double Glaze Window   Two layers of glass set in a window to reduce heat flow in either direction.

Double Hung Window   A window having two vertically sliding sashes, each designed to close a different half of the window.

Drafting   Hand drawings of cabinetry, floor plans, elevations, reflected ceiling plans, and architectural details.

Drafting Board   Smooth board on which paper is placed for making drawings, often can be set at an incline.

Drafting Brush   A handled brush used to clean erasures from your drawing surface.

Drafting Machine   A drafting instrument designed much like a human arm, used for drafting.

Drafting Table   A multipurpose desk that can be used for any kind of drawing, writing, or impromptu sketching on a large sheet of paper, or for reading a large format book or other oversized documents, or for drafting precise technical illustrations.

Dressing   Artistic enhancement of a drawing to further clarify part of the design concept.

Duplex Outlet   Electrical receptacle capable of receiving two plugs.

Dutch Door   Top portion of the door opens and closes independently from the bottom portion of the door.

Eave   The lower edge of the roof that extends beyond the exterior wall.

Electrical Plan   A drafted scale drawing indicating the circuitry and location of electrical elements, including switches and outlets.

Elevation   A drafted scale drawing without being 3-D viewed head on.

Erasing Shield   A small metal template used as a shield to cover areas that are not going to be erased, while showing the areas that will be erased.

Ergonomics   The study of human body movement and its relationship to the space in which it functions.

Fascia   A horizontal board that is used to face a roof edge.

Fenestration   The design and placement of windows in a wall.

Flagstone   Type of flat stone used in landscaping and interiors for walkways and walls.

Floor Plan   Scaled drawing, typically drawn at ¼" to 1'0" scale, indicating walls, windows, electrical outlets, furniture placement, etc.

French Curve   A drafting tool used to draw irregular curves.

French Doors   Two doors closing against each other within a frame.

Gambrel Roof   Ridged roof with two sloped sides, the lower slope having the steeper pitch.

Ganging   Term used to indicate installation of several outlets or switches next to each other.

Guidelines   An exceptionally light line (often created using 4H pencil) used for lining up lettering and numbers and used to form the basis for darker lines.

Hardwood   Wood produced from broad-leafed trees or trees that lose their leaves, such as maple, birch, oak, and walnut.

Head Room   The space between the top of a finished floor and the lowest part of the floor above.

Hearth   Floor surface of a fireplace, either inside or in front of the fireplace; often raised and used for a seat.

Heavy Line Weight   A dark line (often made using an F pencil) used to indicate lines of primary importance in a drawing.

Hopper Window   Hinged at the bottom and opens outward.

HVAC   The abbreviation for heating, ventilation, air-conditioning units.

Insulation   Material used to hinder the transfer of cold, heat, and/or sound from one area to another.

Interior Architecture   Nonresidential interior design that includes remodeling and working with building systems.

Interior Elevation   A straight-on view of the surface of an interior wall or walls of a building.

Interior Trim   Construction term used to denote all interior moldings and baseboards.

Ionic Column   Classical Greek architectural style column with a scroll-shaped capital.

Isometric Drawing   A drawing drafted at a 30-degree angle from the horizontal plane and giving equal emphasis to all visible surfaces; all vertical lines remain vertical and all parallel lines parallel.

Jalousie Window   A window made of long, narrow, horizontal panes of hinged glass.

Jamb   The side and top lining of a doorway, window, or other structural element.

Joist   A horizontal structural component supporting either the floor or ceiling construction.

Junction Box   Container for electrical junctions, usually intended to conceal them from sight.

Landing   A flat area either at the end of stairs or between flights of stairs.

Lath   Thin strip of wood laid parallel and nailed into the studs of a building; walls are plastered over the lath.

Lathwork   Panels or grids constructed with narrow bands of lath; they often are used as screens or decorative elements.

Lattice   A panel made of metal or wood bands interlaced to form a grid with even spacing.

Layout   Defining spaces for specific purposes.

Lead-holder   A device that holds different leads for drawing; also known as a mechanical pencil.

Legend Box   The area containing symbols used in a drawing along with their definitions.

Line Weight   The lightness or darkness of a line drawn in drafting technique.

Lintel   The horizontal member above a door or window or between columns.

Louver   Horizontal slats used in a shutter, screen, or window, sloped to control the movement of light and air.

Louvered Door   Door made up of louvered panels.

Luminaire   A lighting unit consisting of one or more electric lamps with all of the necessary parts and wiring.

Mantel   The ledge above and trim around the opening of a fireplace.

Masonry   Any building material that is bonded together to form a construction element, such as stone, concrete, etc.

Materials and Finishes Board   Boards used to illustrate the materials and finishes selected for a particular design.

Mechanical Pencil   A mechanical devise shaped like a pencil that holds lead for drawing.

Medium Line Weight   Line of secondary significance drawn in a medium weight to designate elements in a drawing.

Millwork   Finish woodwork or carpentry done off site in a mill and delivered to the construction site.

Molding   A trim or finishing piece to cover joists or edges; moldings can be plain or ornate.

Mullion   A vertical piece in an opening dividing the space, used in windows to form divisions.

Muntin   The small bar separating glass panes in a window sash.

Mylar   A transparent film (paper) used in drafting to show layers or different colors possible to use in any given situation.

Newel Post   The post at the last part of a stair railing or balustrade.

Niche   A recess in a wall often used to display art.

Nosing   The rounded edge of a tread. *See also* Bullnose.

Open Floor Plan   The concept in interior design and architectural planning which leaves the spaces open without using walls to delineate space, allowing spaces to be more flexible.

Orthographic Drawings   *See* Plan Drawing, Sections, and Elevation.

Overlay Drafting   Drafting technique that involves placing several layers of tracing paper one on top of the other to develop a drawing concept.

Palladian Window   An arched window with windows on either side.

Paneled Door   A door with formed with rails, stiles, and panels for architectural detailing.

Parallel Rule   A straight-edged rule attached to a drafting table or to a board by wires, used to draw horizontal lines; a parallel rule also is used in conjunction with triangles to draw vertical lines.

Parquet Floor   Hardwood floor laid in small rectangular or square patterns instead of long strips.

Partition Wall   Non-load-bearing interior wall used to divide space.

Pendants   Type of lighting hung from the ceiling, smaller than a chandelier.

Permit   Document issued by local, county, state, or federal government to authorize specific work on a building.

Perspective Sketch   A 3-D sketch or rendering of an interior or exterior space drawn to vanishing points in a perspective manner.

Pilaster   A flat, decorative column that also offers structural support.

Plan Drawing   A flat 2-D scaled drawing of a space looking down directly from above.

Plasterboard   Sheetrock or gypsum board made of pulverized gypsum rock and used to finished the interior walls of a structure; also known as drywall.

Plate Rail   A shelf used to display plates or small collectibles, usually placed above wainscoting.

Plywood   Wood product made of thin sheets of wood glued together in layers.

Poché   Practice of darkening areas on a drawing to aid in the readability of the drawing; the filled or hatched portion of an architectural drawing used to show solid walls.

Pocket Door   A door that slides into a compartment recessed into a wall and thereby hidden from view.

Post   Wood placed vertically as a structural column.

Profiling   Darkening the outline of part of a floor plan to emphasize the shape.

Reflected Ceiling Plan   Drawing drafted to indicate the placement of ceiling fixtures, beams, tiles, and electrical outlets.

Rendering   A term used to denote an elaborate finished drawing used in presentation drafting, an artist's concept or perspective drawing.

Reproduction Drafting   Any form of reproduction to aid in the drafting process.

Reprographics   Includes all techniques used for reproducing two-dimensional original drawings.

Riser   The vertical component of a stair between two treads.

Sandblock   A piece of sandpaper on a wood block used to sharpen pencils to a chisel point.

Scale   The reduced measurement representing a larger measurement, e.g., 1/4" = 1'0".

Schedule   The key or chart that indicates the finish material used on walls, floors, and ceiling and/or lists doors and windows and/or lighting and electrical.

Schematic Drawings   Beginning or initial drawings or sketches drawn freehand to show relationship of areas.

Section   A drawing depicting a structure as if it had been sliced through, showing the internal elements of the structure.

Sconce   A wall-mounted lighting fixture.

Shake Shingles   Roof shingles made of wood, slightly irregular in width, that generally weather to a gray tone in time.

Shed Ceiling   A ceiling that slopes in only one direction.

[GLOSSARY]

Shingles   Wood, tile, or asbestos components used as a finish material on angled roofs.

Shop Drawings   Drawings prepared by the contractor, subcontractor, or manufacturer showing detailed sections of the work to be fabricated and installed.

Sill   The lower structure of an opening, across the bottom, e.g., a door or window sill.

Site Plans   A drawing that shows where a building is situated on the land or lot, including the legal boundaries and hookups.

Sketch   A quick and sometimes rough drawing or illustration of a proposed space or detail of a given space.

Soffit   The underside of a roof overhang or of another building component, such as an arch, stairway, or cornice, often used as a location for mounting lighting fixtures.

Space Planning   The process of organizing spaces to meet certain needs, properly allocating spaces to create workable floor plans.

Spiral Staircase   Staircase working similar to a corkscrew.

Stairway   One or more flights of stairs with landings.

Stair Tread   The horizontal surface of a stair run.

Stipple   The technique of drawing dots in order to define an area in a drawing, e.g., to indicate carpet in a drawing.

Stool   The horizontal interior trim component of the casing below a window.

Studs (or Stud Wall)   The vertical constituent making up the main framework of a wall.

Surround   The noncombustible material separating the opening of the fireplace from the wall and/or mantel.

Technical Drawings   Floor plans, elevations, and detailed drawings showing architectural detail.

Title Block   The part of a drawing that lists the general information about the project—client name, project name, date, scale, type of drawing.

Toe Space (or Toe Kick)   Recess at the base of cabinetry.

Tread   The horizontal section of the stair one steps on.

T-Square   Drafting implement in the shape of a T, used to draft horizontal lines or used as a base to use triangles and other lines.

Universal Design   Approach to design creating spaces that can be accessed and utilized by all individuals, regardless of age, size, abilities, or disabilities.

Vellum   The grade of drafting paper, thicker than tracing paper, often used for presentation drawings.

Vertical Lines   Up and down lines that raise the eye and bring decorum and formality into interiors.

Wainscot   Wooden wall paneling on the lower portion of an interior wall, the finish of which generally is different from the portion directly above, e.g., wood versus plaster.

Water Closet   A room containing a toilet; a bathroom; a toilet.

Windowsill   The horizontal ridge or shelf beneath the glass, usually part of the window frame.

Working Drawings   The final drawings used to obtain bids and create a contract.

Zero Clearance Fireplace   A fireplace unit that can be placed into combustible walls allowing no clearance.